To: -
Rec.

MW01205749

Acts 1: 4-5
Receive Power
Acts 1: 8

Charles E. Cilley

NATIONAL ASSOCIATION OF
UNITED METHODIST EVANGELISTS
CAROL STREAM, IL., 60188-2485
Phone (630) 668- 1430   Mobile (630) 207- 3415
e-mail- cmcilley@flash.net

AZ- Oct. 15, 2007 – April 29, 2008 (602) 840- 4366

CHARLES E. CILLEY, SR.
ASSOCIATE EVANGELIST

Who Needs a Comforter?

by

Charles E. Tilley, Sr.

authorHOUSE®

AuthorHouse™
1663 Liberty Drive, Suite 200
Bloomington, IN 47403
www.authorhouse.com
Phone: 1-800-839-8640

First published by AuthorHouse 7/2/2007

ISBN: 978-1-4343-1753-7 (sc)

Library of Congress Control Number: 2007904095

*Printed in the United States of America
Bloomington, Indiana*

This book is printed on acid-free paper.

Acknowldgement

Special mention is made of my loving daughter, Ruth Ann Cilley Reynolds. She looked at my first manuscript and suggested a more flowing, easier to read story. She also understands computers better than her Dad.

In spite of personal situations that have required many hours of her time for family and professional matters, she has persisted to the end. She has been a great encouragement to me when at times this project appeared to be too much for a new comer to the authorship field.

It is with extreme gratitude to her, for her undying devotion and love, that I say:

THANK YOU, RUTH !!

and

THANK YOU, LORD !!

Dedication

This first volume of *Who Needs a Comforter* is dedicated to all the individuals who find themselves in their own individual "prison". Hopefully, by the time you finish reading this volume, you will understand what I mean by the phrase 'their own individual "prison" '.

Such a person may fall into any one or more of the following situations.

- A relative of a suicide victim
- A person living with suicidal tendencies
- An abused person- verbally, sexually, physically and/or self abused
- A person with an addiction such as alcohol, drugs, money, sex, self-image and/or occupation

Over the past 20+ years, I have had the opportunity and privilege to encounter people in all of these situations. Some have been comforted and some have not. 'Why' one person may be comforted and another may not be comforted is one of the mysteries of life.

My prayer is that you will find comfort; I pray that you find your Comforter!

Table of Contents

Preface to the Book

When the Lord placed the thought of writing a book on the Holy Spirit into to my mind, I immediately asked, "Why me Lord?" Some of the answers I received are contained in the book. Some I am still working on. Nevertheless, I would like to share a brief summary of some of my key thoughts.

- A person is not too old or too young to be a comforter.
- Most people have burdens. (I will refer to them as their "Jerusalem")
- Most people desire peace in the world and in their life.
- Most people have a fear of the unknown.
- Experience counts!
- We all can be comforters (ministers) to someone - we do not have to be clergy.
- It is time for the laity of the church to be more supportive of the clergy.
- God is faithful.

On an ABC television program entitled *Resurrection*, a couple of comments hit home.

First, it was stated that in their right mind, many people want to believe the grave is not the end. This reminded me of a saying, the only difference between a rut and a grave is the dimension. Perhaps the producer is in the rut and they do not believe in eternal life. Or perhaps they don't know what to believe. As a born-again believer, I definitely believe the grave is not the end - it is just the beginning. Actually, it is the end of this life on earth, but it can be a glorious GRADUATION to life eternal. IF … and this is a big IF, you accept Jesus Christ as your Lord and Savior. Read on to find how easy it is have such a GRADUATION. It doesn't take four years of college or a lot of money! Many people don't know what to believe. This is another reason for my book.

Second, two billion Christians are caught up in the power of their experiences. This hits the backbone of this book. Again, I suggest you read on to find out more about the POWER and a few of the EXPERIENCES that I have had the privilege to witness in my life. You may decide if I am one of the two billion Christians who are caught up in the power of their experiences or just caught up in THE Power. Whichever you decide, the power of experiences or THE Power, it's your decision. You have the power! However, I MUST hasten to add that Jesus' POWER, through the Holy Spirit, is available to ALL people regardless of age, intelligence, background, culture, nationality, gender, race, or wealth.

For more information about the program *Resurrection*, go to <u>www.ABCnewsstore.com</u>. This program was viewed May 20, 2005, on ABC in Chicago.

While I have been contemplating this book, many interesting things have happened in my life and in the world. In my life, many trials and tribulations have come my way. These trials and tribulations have been physical, emotional and spiritual. I have been blessed to be a team member on 19 week-end experiences with Aldersgate Renewal Ministries (ARM). See chapter 4 for more about ARM. I have attended eight annual Holy Spirit conferences of the United Methodist Church. During 2004, I read over 25 books, primarily religious in nature. Before that time, I could hardly read one chapter without falling asleep. God is amazing in many ways!

In the world, the World Trade Center in New York City was destroyed on September 11, 2001. A tsunami hit the Indian Ocean area in 2003. In February 2003, Kenneth E. Hagin had a vision before going to be with the Heavenly Father in September of the same year. In 2004, Oral Roberts had a vision concerning the second coming of the Lord. This event piqued Kenneth Copeland's interests enough that he had Oral Roberts on his TV program for four days and then spent six days with Billye Brim, Gloria Copeland and Kenneth Copeland commenting on the meaning of this vision for the world, the Jews, and the Church. See Appendix J for further details. In 2005-2007, many devastating hurricanes, floods, fires and earthquakes have hit throughout the world.

Pastor John Hagee of Cornerstone Church in San Antonio, TX has written a book entitled *Jerusalem Countdown*. He talks about EMP (electro motive pulse) which, when and if it becomes a reality, could be a major factor in the end times.

In my mind, all of these happenings in the world dovetail together to give us a real need for the Comforter. I hasten to emphasize a comment that is made early in my book and repeated several times. Don't accept everything that anyone says without careful analysis.

Oral Roberts claimed that God told him, "My people are not ready for the second coming of my Son" (See Appendix J). I believe that the basic concept of this book is extremely pertinent to the world today and the near future. After you finish reading this first volume of *Who Needs a Comforter*, please send your comments or questions to the author at the publisher's address. Also, watch for Volumes 2 and 3 of *Who Needs a Comforter*, which will hopefully, be published soon.

CHAPTER 1 –
Why?

Do not accept everything that anyone says without careful analysis. Consider your thoughts, your understanding, your principles, and your opinions. Most importantly, consider how others' words, ideas and thoughts line up with the Word of God.

All books, including this one, should be critically examined with these thoughts in mind. We each have something unique to offer the world. I hope that you will find something special in this book.

Why Do We Need Another Book?

Many people have written about God and His works in this world. Bookstores overflow with books that beg to be read. So why this book?

First, experience counts. God has spoken to my heart and told me to share my experiences with you. Many experiences, both from others lives and from mine, are included on these pages. But, your experiences count too. Share them! Tell someone! You are not too old or too young to have experiences. Share your experiences with others.

Secondly, we are all ministers. You don't have to have Reverend by your name to be a blessing to others. By sharing your experiences or your story, you can minister to others.

Thirdly, we all have burdens, some heavier than others. Regardless of their weight, they are our personal burdens. They are our crosses to bear. This book will give you comfort IF you will release your burden.

Fourth, we all want peace in our lives. But, how can this be achieved? Read on! Also, many of us are fearful of the unknown. We hide in our houses; we stay sheltered in our ignorance.

God said,

> *"My people are destroyed from lack of knowledge."*
> *Hosea 4:6 NIV.*

Lastly, God is faithful. Just as the sun rises and sets every day regardless whether it is cloudy or sunny, from our viewpoint, God is faithful to be with us during our times of trials and tribulations as well as our times of joy and celebration. He will show up when you least expect Him. Call upon the Lord, He said He would never leave us or forsake us.

It is true that many excellent books have been written concerning the Holy Spirit. However, clergy wrote most of those. This book is written by a layperson, a member of the United Methodist Church and an ordinary person wishing to share God's message with you.

Why A Comforter?

The idea of a comforter began to grow in my mind beginning in 1999. I had a knee replacement, which proceeded very well for the first year. Then my knee became infected and I had to have three operations in four months. Not a great experience but one I needed to live through. God had His plan! My replacement knee was removed, a spacer put in while the infection healed and a new knee was put in place. During that time I couldn't exercise or move around as I was used to, which caused my physical and social circulation to deteriorate. Just sitting around made me cold and I needed some help; I needed comfort. My wife found a comforter. It was an old soft warm comforter. Just what I needed! Then she gave me a fancy, electric comforter. You know, there really was no difference between the two, until I plugged in the fancy one. Connected to a power source, the electric comforter made me warm all over. My feet stayed warm; my knee stayed warm; I was comforted.

Many of us remember the summer of 2003 when the northeast United States experienced a massive power failure. We realized how much we benefit from an invisible resource, electricity. The results of electricity are usually good. It makes our microwaves work; we push a button, the TV goes on; flip a switch and the lights shine all because we have an invisible power source, called electricity. Could electricity be like the invisible source that provides us with energy? Could our God be like electricity, giving us invisible power? Once we are connected, we are comforted.

Years ago, a two-prong plug was common on all electrical plugs. However, the electrical industry made a change for the better. They created the three-prong plug. This change came about for safety reasons, to ground the electrical system more securely. These old two-prong plugs remind me of the way that many Christians see God. I believe many of today's Christians talk only about God the Father and God the Son, Jesus Christ. This is like the two-pronged electrical plug. They have forgotten the third prong, the Holy Spirit. Over the years, many "Christians" have thought the theology and attention to the Holy Spirit would be divisive and therefore, many didn't want to talk about it. But thankfully, today, many Christians are talking about the third prong of Christianity, the Holy Spirit.

Why Three Prongs?

Remember why we now have the three-pronged electrical plugs? Right, for safety and a better grounding of the electrical system. In the same way, many Christians have started using the three-prong approach to their faith. They talk about God the Father, God the Son - Jesus Christ and God the Holy Spirit. Because of this, Christians are better grounded. They have a stronger, more secure basis for their understanding of theology, their understanding of God and of the scriptures. You too, can become better grounded. You can have the three-prongs of God and celebrate His great grounding power through the third prong - the Holy Spirit.

> *"But you will receive power when the Holy Spirit comes on you; and you will be my witnesses in Jerusalem, and in all Judea and Samaria, and to the ends of the earth." (Acts 1: 8 NIV)*

Jesus tells His disciples:

> *"All this I have spoken while still with you. But the Counselor, the Holy Spirit, whom the Father will send in my name, will teach you all things and*

will remind you of everything I have said to you."
(John 14:25-26, NIV)

In the same way, when we learn more about the Holy Spirit, we will have another helper, a Counselor, a Teacher, a Comforter, to assist us in our daily lives. He will also help us have a firmer foundation in the scriptures. After all, He is the author of the Word!

Continuing on in John 14, Jesus says:

"Peace I leave with you; my peace I give you. I do not give to you as the world gives. Do not let your hearts be troubled and do not be afraid."
(John 14:27 NIV)

The world does not give us peace. One of the benefits of a relationship with the Holy Spirit, as claimed by many of the people I have spoken to, is experiencing a peace which they have rarely experienced before. This peace possibly was experienced when they accepted Jesus Christ as their Lord and Savior. God's peace, the peace of the Holy Spirit, filled them again when they rested in the Spirit.

This book is more than a book of experiences. It is full of comments, questions, suggestions and "how to" ideas about becoming a better friend and a comforter to others. God is the ultimate Comforter but you can be a comforter too. If you find this book meaningful, and I pray that you do, then the time and expense that it has taken for me to write it will be well worth it. God the Father, the Son, and the Holy Spirit is the peace and the comfort that we all seek.

CHAPTER 2 –
Meet the author and The Author

Who Is The Author Of This Book?

The Webster dictionary describes an author as [1] one that originates or creates or [2] one that writes or composes. I would like to share with you my testimony and background as the author, one who writes, of this book. Then I'll share my thoughts on the Author, one who originates or creates, of THE BOOK.

Born in Concord, New Hampshire in 1928, I was the youngest of three boys in a typical family of that era. My father died when I was 10 years old, and my mother raised us in a single-parent family. That term, single-parent family was not used often in the 1930s and we didn't talk about it as much in those days as we do today.

As a Boy Scout, I had the honor of being a page at the United Nations Monetary Conference in Bretton Woods, New Hampshire. Our senator from New Hampshire selected me for this honor.

After graduating from Concord High School in 1946, I studied at the University of New Hampshire and graduated in 1950 with a Bachelor of Science degree in Chemistry. I worked for Hercules Powder Company and

Masonite Corporation as a chemist for 20 years. For the last 30+ years, I've worked in real estate and insurance.

In 1948, while working at York Beach, Maine I found the jewel of my life. She was a waitress at a local hotel and I was the "Cilley" soda jerk at a very popular snack shop, ice cream parlor and bakery called "The Goldenrod". After three summers of romancing at this popular beach resort town, Marjorie Johnson and I were married. We are the proud parents of three girls and one boy. Currently we have twelve grandchildren and one great-grandchild. During those 30+ years, we moved from Delaware to Michigan to California and finally to Illinois, where we currently live. That is the physical side of me.

Spiritually, but just as important and possibly more important, I have a different story. I was baptized at the Advent Christian Church in Concord, New Hampshire when I was nine. Total water immersion was a common method of baptism in that church. I was baptized in this way and I was a good "Christian" in the following years. I attended many churches including a small country chapel, was a Sunday school teacher and superintendent, and had many other responsibilities. When I was 50, I received the "Baptism of the Holy Spirit" at a United Methodist Men's Conference at Lake Geneva, Wisconsin. The idea of baptism of the Holy Spirit may be a new subject to many of you and I will explain it more later in the book. You could say that I had been wandering in the wilderness for 41 years, from age 9 to 50. However, I consider myself fortunate as I was in good company with Moses and the Israelites! Since that conference at Lake Geneva and the experience of being baptized of the Holy Spirit, I have never been the same.

> *"Therefore, if anyone is in Christ, he is a new creation; the old has gone, the new has come!" (II Corinthians 5:17 NIV)*

God gave me many activities to utilize my new found Spirit. He was teaching me how to be a comforter to others. By working with Project Understanding Bail Project, Full Gospel Business Men Fellowship International, Luis Palau "Say Yes Chicago" campaign and Straight Talk, God began His lessons in comforting. He continued His lessons in comforting when I attended the Promise Keepers conference in 1996 and several years since then. Most recently, the opportunity to be a comforter has developed with Brothers in Christ at my local church and Aldersgate Renewal Ministries, which is the charismatic arm of the United Methodist Church. Through this ongoing process, God has taught me to be a comforter to others. But, God does not discriminate or show favoritism. What he has done for me He will do for you, if you believe and have faith in Him.

> *"Then Peter began to speak: 'I now realize how true it is that God does not show favoritism but accepts men from every nation who fear him and do what is right.' "* *(Acts 10:34-35 NIV)*

While we can be a comforter to others, family, friends, relatives, fellow workers or even strangers, the ultimate and perfect comforter is the Holy Spirit. Remember that the Holy Spirit is the third-prong of the Trinity. The Holy Spirit provides the grounding that we all need in our daily lives.

Who Is The Author Of The Book?

Throughout history there has always been and will always be, great discussions about who is the author of the Bible. Remember the second definition for author? One who originates or creates. My belief about the Author of the Bible has two parts. First, the Bible was written down by human beings. However, I believe the Spirit of God inspired those human beings. This belief is supported in the following passages.

> *"All Scripture is God-breathed and is useful for teaching, rebuking, correcting and training in righteousness, so that the man of God may be thoroughly equipped for every good work".* *(II Timothy 3:16-17 NIV)*

"But it is the Spirit in a man, the breath of the Almighty, that gives him understanding." (Job 32:8 NIV)

Secondly, many of the common threads throughout the Word could not have happened by coincidence. Hence, I believe the Holy Spirit, the third-prong of the Trinity, is the Author of the Bible.

If we wish to understand the Word better than we ever have in the past, or even now in the present, the best way to do this is to meet the Author. This book will help you meet the Holy Spirit. How exciting to have the opportunity to meet the great Author of THE BOOK!

CHAPTER 3 –
The "Whys" of Life

Life holds many whys. Why is there suffering? Why do we have sickness? Why do we need surgeries and hospitalization, as I did? Why is there division within families, between people or between nations? Why is there division between and within denominations? Why do we need renewal and revival? I am sure that you can ask many other whys.

Why Is There Suffering?

Recently while reading *A Step Further* by Joni Eareckson Tada and Steve Estes, several comments of Joni's seem to "hit the nail on the head" for the question of suffering. I would refer you to Tada/Estes book, *A Step Further*, for several comments of Joni's concerning this subject, page 167 in particular.

Joni makes many references to J.I. Packer's book titled *Knowing God,* which had many answers for her that were life-changing. Joni indicates that led her to searching the Bible, where she got further answers of her own.

Personally, I agree that is an excellent suggestion, SEARCH THE BIBLE FOR SOME ANSWERS AND DEVELOP OPINIONS OF YOUR OWN.

The great book of Job is the most outstanding example of suffering. Even though God permits suffering to happen to us just like He did to Job, I believe:

- God knows what He is doing,
- God has a plan for each one of us – particularly IF we are a follower of His,
- God is in control.

IF we put our TRUST in Him, He will see us through!

I suggest that every reader of this book take time to read the complete book of Job.

If God were to explain any and all of the great mysteries of suffering, division, personalities, cultures, etc. could we comprehend what He was saying? Possibly, we could understand a small portion of it. Isn't it like a jigsaw puzzle or a foreign language? With a jigsaw puzzle, it is difficult to see the complete picture until ALL of the pieces are in place. Not only in place but they must be in the <u>proper</u> or <u>correct</u> place. Likewise, knowing just a small amount of a foreign language does not give us the ability to carry on a fluent conversation with a native of that language. In order to have a meaningful communication with the native we MUST study their language extensively. So it is with God and the mysteries of life. We need to study His manual of life - the Bible - and apply its principles and promises on a daily basis.

This whole question of "why" reminds me of a saying: *"If I understood all the whys of life, I would be God, and since I am not God, I do not have to be concerned about all the whys of life."* (Author Unknown)

Why Do We Have Sickness?

(Why do we need surgeries and hospitalization, as I did?)

Being hospitalized four times in seventeen months, caused me to ask the question, Why? many times. My wife helped me see and often reminded me about why I was there.

One time as I was on my way to one of many tests, I started talking with the transport specialist (formerly called an orderly) about the church that he attended. This began a very interesting discussion, which led him to begin searching his relationship with God. In other words, a seed, or thought was planted. Someone else will water it. Someone else will harvest the fruit. We must all be faithful to our calling. Are you a sower, a cultivator (or comforter) and/or a harvester? ALL are needed!

Another time I was sharing God's word through my testimony with one of the nurses. It was 10pm and all was relatively quiet on the floor. After a word of prayer with her, she left my room only to return a few minutes later with another staff member. Both people were led to a closer walk with the Lord through that experience. My wife often said that anyone who walked through my door would be ministered to. I guess that was *why* I was there.

However, ministering takes many forms. As much as I love to minister to others, sometimes I needed ministering. One day while I was still in the hospital, a pastor friend with three of his prayer warriors came to visit me. They had driven two hours just to visit me and hold a private worship service in my room. They read Scripture to me, we sang songs, the pastor had a brief message and we prayed. During the prayer time, I felt a hand on the right side of my chest. I thanked my pastor friend for the prayer and for his comforting touch. The pastor's comforting touch? My friend was confused. He had not touched me! Then who had? I believe that the Lord touched me. HE had touched me! Immediately we sang "He Touched Me" by William Gaither:

> *Shackled by a heavy burden, neath a load of guilt and shame, then the hand of Jesus touched me, and now I am no longer the same. He touched me, O he touched me, and O the joy that floods my soul! Something happened, and now I know, he touched me and made me whole. (United Methodist Hymnal, 1989, p. 367)*

Why Is There Division?

(WITHIN FAMILIES; BETWEEN PEOPLE; BETWEEN NATIONS; BETWEEN DENOMINA-TIONS and WITHIN DENOMINATIONS?)

No matter which type of division we are talking about, it has often been said that we are not on the same playing field. Our family backgrounds, traditions, and cultures vary. We all experience life in many different ways. Our beliefs and experiences create differences. Although we celebrate the differences in each other, these differences often lead to disagreement, confusion and uneasiness in communications. When I was growing up, I used to hear people say that there was a Generational Gap. I seriously doubt that such a gap ever existed. Instead, I believe it was a Communication Gap. Even today, over half a century later, a Communication Gap still exists. When we play by different sets of rules, communication is difficult.

In other words, if one person is playing baseball and following all the baseball rules but the other person is playing football and following all the football rules, on the same field, confusion will occur. If the rules change to make baseball like football or football like baseball then neither game is ever the same. Agreement becomes difficult. Life works the same way. When people from two cultures marry, adjustments must occur. Each person brings their unique background and experiences to the marriage to create a new union. Division can occur unless people are open and understanding of each other's uniqueness.

This is also true of differences within denominations. If there is not a foundation of the basic premises or truth, then communication and agreement are difficult. I have heard many questions. Does it really matter what you call God? Is there only one way to God? Does God love everyone? Can God really forgive me? Will everyone have eternal life? Does God let bad things happen to good people? All of these questions can be answered with YES, but some will dispute this answer. It will cause much discussion with many different opinions and in some cases, hostility. In the world today where there is no foundational agreement, hostility, or at least disagreement and division, often erupts. This can be seen in alternative lifestyles, bi-racial marriages, how we use time, our priorities, political and religious views, human rights, and our view of God. Our foundational religious beliefs can create divisions or at least discussion. For example, what is the difference between "Religion" and "Christianity"? For me it is very basic BUT some will disagree. Once again, as I mentioned in the beginning of the book, I encourage everyone to analyze critically all things in print. Just because it is published does not mean it is the only truth.

I believe:

<u>Religion</u> is a belief in a doctrine and

<u>Christianity</u> is a personal relationship with Jesus Christ.

People can have Religion but not Christianity. People can believe in Christianity but not *have* Christianity. Do you *have* Christianity or just Religion?

Our priorities also speak to our foundational beliefs. Where is your priority?

"The Rookie Demon" read by Tony Evans on an Urban Alternative radio program speaks to a very common attitude about the subject of priority.

"The rookie demon was just learning the ropes. He wanted to impress Lucifer, so he went to Lucifer and said. 'I'm going to destroy a bunch of Christians for you. I want to be your main man.'

"So with Lucifer's blessing the Rookie went out. He came back dejected. The Devil said, 'What's wrong?'

"The Rookie said, 'I tried to tell the Christians there was no sin. They didn't buy it.'

"The Devil said, 'You can just look at the world and know that's not the case.'

"The Rookie said, 'Give me another chance! I will try something else.'

"He came back dejected again. The Devil said, 'What's wrong?'

"The Rookie said, 'I tried to tell them there was no God. That didn't work either.'

"The Devil said, 'It is no wonder they didn't accept that. After all, they committed their lives to God, so it is hard to convince them to believe that.'

"The Rookie said, 'Give me one more chance.' However, this time he came back in tears.

"The Devil said, 'What's wrong?'

"The Rookie said, 'I told them there was no Resurrection.'

"The Devil said, 'That's not going to work as the whole Christian faith is predicated on the resurrection.'

"The Rookie said, 'How come you have been so successful?'

"The Devil said, 'Sit down, my boy, let me explain something. You can't tell them there is no sin; or there is no God or there is no resurrection. The reason I have been so successful all these years is that I tell them there is "No hurry". I get them so wrapped up into the affairs of this world that they don't deny spiritual things, they just delay them. Getting Christians to delay things, I have been able to enlarge my kingdom in hell enormously. Christians are quick to say, tomorrow; next week; or next year."

We all have the same 24 hours per day. We can do with these hours as we please. God gave all of us free will to choose how we use our 24 hours. However, this freedom may not be available to all because man has set his priorities above God's priorities. Our present circumstances and/or the consequences of our previous behavior may have an over-riding influence on this freedom.

Regardless, whether you are living under a dictatorship, in a physical prison or an "individual prison" (of your own making) where you are restricted, you still have a mind of your own. Governments can establish guidelines for our outer conditions but only you can control your inner soul and spiritual conditions

Is there division so the Devil can survive? No, the devil survives because both man and Lucifer rebelled against God. Originally, Lucifer, an angel of God, thought, through his prideful attitude, that he could do a better job on running the world than God was doing. Lucifer tried to take control of the world. Temporarily, God has allowed him through the original sin of Adam and Eve, to be the prince of this world. Today some human beings still believe they could do a better job of running the world than God is doing. This attitude reminds me of a reading that Paul Harvey gave on one of his radio programs. The reading is entitled "If I Were the Devil" and goes like this:

"I would gain control of the most powerful nation in the world; would delude their minds into thinking that they had come from man's effort, instead of God's blessings;

"I would promote an attitude of loving things and using people, instead of the other way around;

"I would dupe entire states into relying on gambling for their state revenue;

"I would convince people that character is not an issue when it comes to leadership;

"I would make it legal to take the life of unborn babies;

"I would make it socially acceptable to take one's own life, and invent machines to make it convenient;

"I would cheapen human life as much as possible so that the life of animals are valued more than human beings;

"I would take God out of the schools, where even the mention of His name was grounds for a lawsuit;

"I would come up with drugs that sedate the mind and target the young, and I would get sports heroes to advertise them;

"I would get control of the media, so that every night I would pollute the mind of every family member for my agenda;

"I would attack the family, the backbone of any nation;

"I would make divorce acceptable and easy, even fashionable. If the family crumbles, so does the nation;

"I would compel people to express their depraved fantasies on canvas and movie screens, and I would call it art;

"I would convince the world that people are born homosexuals and that their lifestyles should be accepted and marveled;

"I would convince the people that right and wrong are determined by a few who call themselves authorities and refer to their agenda as politically correct;

"I would persuade people that the church is irrelevant and out of date, and the Bible is for the naïve;

"I would dull the minds of Christians, and make them believe that prayer is not important, and that faithfulness and obedience are optional;

"I guess I would leave things pretty much the way they are."

This is a powerful explanation of how the devil has control of the world. Pretty realistic, isn't it? This story relates how man has let the devil take over the present world.

Are you happy with YOUR present world?

Some will say "Yes"; some will say, "No". I say, "No", and I believe it is time for revival and renewal.

Why Do We Need Renewal And Revival?

What is meant by a renewal and revival? Are they the same thing? Do we use these words to mean the same event or happening?

A dictionary definition is:

RENEWAL is to make new again or to restore to the former state. REVIVAL, in a religious context, is an awakening in a church in matters relating to a personal relationship with Jesus Christ. It also means a service or series of services for affecting a religious awakening.

Do people use renewal as the politically correct word for revival? I think they do. Have you ever experienced revival, either individually (you personally) or corporately, as a church?

Over the period of many years, there have been profound revivals such as Azusa Street in the early 1900s and Toronto Airport Blessing of the late 1900s. Many excellent books on the revivals of the world have been written and I will not attempt to summarize them. If you are interested in the history of revivals including the Azusa Street and Toronto Airport Blessing, the internet can provide you with a plethora of information.

In 2000, I developed and presented an advanced course for the Lay Speaker's Academy in the Aurora District, Northern Illinois Conference of the United Methodist Church. This course is titled, "Lay Speaker's Role in Renewal/Revival Worship in the Local Church".

Remembering we all are ministers, or comforters, this course could be called "<u>Your</u> Role in Renewal/Revival in the Local Church". BUT- How? Each of the 6 sessions provide hands-on skills to develop spiritual growth (revival). Learn by DOING IT!

See Appendix F for an outline of this course.

CHAPTER 4 –
What Makes A Person?

Experiences, thoughts, beliefs.
Without these, are we really people?

Many experiences have contributed to who I am. Six organizations have consumed much of my energy for the past 25 to 30 years. Each organization has been an important building block for who I am at this point of my life. They have contributed to my experience, thoughts, and beliefs.

Project Understanding Bail Project, Inc

For the past 30 years, my wife and I have been involved with the organization Project Understanding Bail Project, Inc. (PUBP). Project Understanding is a not-for-profit organization in DuPage County, Illinois that assists people released from jail or prison. Many people do not understand the difference between jail and prison. Jail is usually a local city or county facility and holds an individual for up to one year. If an individual were incarcerated longer than one year, he or she would be held in a state or federal prison.

Many organizations minister to people while they are incarcerated in jails or prisons. However, very few assist people after release. While both ministries are very important, I believe a greater need exists for one-on-one assistance after release. When an individual returns to the outside world, he or she faces huge challenges. As the old saying goes, when the rubber hits the road the challenges rise up. Returning to society, particularly after long term incarceration, is very, very difficult. Through Project Understanding, individuals have received a wide variety of services and ministry. We have helped with clothing, furniture, temporary housing including a "half-way" house, obtaining employment, finances including budget training, transportation, getting to court; counseling for the individual and family and obtaining a car. A car is almost a necessity in a suburban area such as DuPage County, Illinois. Of course, it is mandatory for the PUBP clients to have a valid driver's license and auto insurance. Normally our clients do not have a newer car, which would require full coverage auto insurance. If someone donates a newer car to the Project, we would usually sell it and buy two or three older vehicles. Unfortunately, if their car broke down or just stopped running, they would just leave it by the side of the road. This probably comes from a lack of knowledge about what to do with it or a lack of money to fix it. Either way, it creates a problem for the PUBP. Since we always retain the title, we are called to pickup the car. Sometimes this means large towing and storage expenses. If the vehicle is not worth picking up and the client has not been in touch with us, we will give the title to the towing company and let them junk the vehicle.

Many times the clients expect everything handed to them. One of the first comments that I say to an individual is, "All the help in the world is not worth a darn unless you are willing to help yourself." We cannot force anyone to change their ways, it is necessary for them to make the choice to change. Also, I would tell them that we can drop them just as fast as we came to their assistance if they did not demonstrate a desire to help themselves. In the early years, more people were interested in helping themselves than they are today. As a matter-of-fact, I have discussed this with many social workers and they agree that many people today are more interested in a hand out than in helping themselves.

If you are reading this book, I believe you are not one who is just interested in a hand out. I encourage you to keep reading and hopefully, find the answers to your questions. If you don't have a question, that's ok. Sometimes we find the answer before the question. How? Just keep on reading. I may not know the answer to your question, but I do know the one who has the answer -- Jesus Christ!

Project Understanding has given me many interesting experiences. I hope I will be able to share more of them in volumes 2 and 3 of Who Needs a Comforter. Someone once said, "We will always have the poor with us, but it does not have to be the same individual all the time." When assisting the homeless and recently released, I have used this phrase quite often. No one needs to stay in the position he finds himself in today, however, he does need to be willing to make a choice to change. I believe the best way to do this is through healing of memories.

Over the years, we have assisted a wide range of individuals, both male and female, who have been incarcerated for a variety of activities from vagrancy to murder. Most of the individuals had been released from the county jail, some from the state prison and a few from federal prison. Over all, the recidivism, or return rate through PUBP is just the opposite of the normal recidivism rate under the "rehabilitation" program of the state or county. Normally 80% of the people released from jail or prison return. Whereas, with the intervention of Project Understanding 80% stay out of jail or prison. Project Understanding works!

We have been asked many times what percentage of people are in jail or prison because of drugs or alcohol. My answer has always been 90 to 95%. It is practically impossible or at least meaningless to talk with individuals when they are under the influence. These people must become sober before lasting change can occur. Another group of people that is very difficult to work with is the mentally ill. These people present a different set of challenges. However, regardless of the condition we find ourselves in, we ALL need a comforter. Who is your comforter? Can you turn to your Comforter for peace and guidance?

It is reported that Mother Theresa said, "No one should ever die without being held in the arms of someone who loves them." I remember approaching a person who appeared troubled. I said to her, "God loves you and so do I love you, as a Child of God." She broke down in tears and we had a wonderful time of sharing. You never know the pain that another person carries inside until you show a little LOVE.

Love overcomes!!

Full Gospel Business Men Fellowship International (FGBMFI)

The Full Gospel Business Men's Fellowship International is an organization that began in Los Angeles, California in 1951. The website states, "It was thrust into global ministry by prophetic visions and prophecy" (www. fgbmfi.org). This organization has thousands of local chapters in 132 countries. Men meet for breakfast, lunch, or dinner and a time of fellowship, outreach and personal ministry. The Fellowship members make a "commitment to spread the Good News of Christ through the effective and powerful worldwide ministries" (www.fgbmfi.org) of the chapters.

I became involved with FGBMFI when the group was meeting at a local bowling alley on Saturday mornings. After several years, we moved to Denny's restaurant nearby. We had a separate room in the back where 15 to 20 men attended a breakfast meeting, every Saturday mornings. Throughout the years of my involvement with this organization, I was a Field Representative and President of the local chapter. It was at this restaurant that I first experienced praying for someone to receive the baptism of the Holy Spirit, as manifested by resting in the Spirit. (Chapters 5 and 12 give more details on "Baptism of the Holy Spirit, as manifested by resting in the Spirit".)

It was also at this restaurant that I prayed for Glen's healing. Glen had a spinal cord injury due to an accident and he had developed severe ulcers. He explained that many people with spinal cord injuries also develop ulcers. Glen's ulcers were healed during one of our Saturday morning prayer times. Although I prayed for the healing of his spinal cord, that never occurred. When Glen traveled to the rehab center in Chicago, he shared with the people at the center that his ulcers had been cured. Someone asked him what church he attended. He replied that he went to the Church of Denny's. Sometimes the only church that some people attend might be an organization such as FGBMFI.

Why are some people healed of one illness or injury and not another? Why do some receive healing and others do not? Why did God choose Glen and not others? God does the healing and not us. Let God do His work and let us do ours. We are just instruments in God's hands. If we are believers, we do have the responsibility of praying with and for all of our brothers and sisters in Christ and any human being who is willing to have someone pray with them. The FGBMFI has made a powerful impact on many people.

It was through FGBMFI that I met Jerry McMahon, a former regional vice president of the organization. Jerry told me, what I believe to be a very profound statement, which I have used many times. It is:

"I will not defend or debate the Scriptures with you, I will let the Holy Spirit do it for you; the same as He has done with me."

Straight Talk

Many years ago, Luis Palau came to Chicago for a "Say Yes, Chicago" campaign. This campaign was an evangelistic activity of several days involving many churches and denominations throughout the Chicago area. I attended an organizational meeting as a representative of our local church. Each county surrounding Chicago created a similar group to assist in this campaign. Following the campaign three counties joined and organized a group called Straight Talk. This group has carried on the ministry that was started under the "Say Yes, Chicago" campaign. The Straight Talk group meets two or three times a year in each county. Speakers are invited, primarily from the sports field, to share their personal life experience including how they came to know Christ. Just like FGBMFI, Straight Talk goes to the people instead of waiting for them to come to church. Straight Talk encourages men to take their faith and beliefs into the business world. It is very encouraging when one sees fellow men taking their faith and beliefs into the work arena. For some reason men normally hesitate to mix faith and belief with their occupation. MEN-Let's go for IT!!

Promise Keepers

As stated in their web site (www.promisekeepers.org) Mission Statement:

"Promise Keepers is dedicated to igniting and uniting men to be passionate followers of Jesus Christ through the effective communication of the 7 Promises. A sovereign move of God's Spirit is stirring the hearts of men. In a world of negotiable values, confused identities and distorted priorities, men are encountering God's Word, embracing their identities as His sons and investing meaningful relationships with God, their families and each other. Clearly, Christian men have an unprecedented opportunity to seize this moment and make a difference for Jesus Christ. We believe that God wants to use Promise Keepers as a spark in His hand to ignite a nationwide movement calling men from all denominational, ethnic, and cultural backgrounds to reconciliation, discipleship and godliness."

One year I attended a Promise Keepers event in Milwaukee, Wisconsin where they had a sign posted saying "EVs NEEDED". EVs are the Evangelist Volunteers who wear a large orange circle with big letters EV on them. They are the ones who come forward when an altar call is given. They pray with the participants of the conference who have felt the pull or call of the Holy Spirit. I went to the volunteers' area and spoke with the person in charge. I asked, "Is it okay if people fall under the Spirit when I pray with them?" Some organizations do not want this manifestation of the baptism of the Holy Spirit to be demonstrated at their meetings. He responded that it was okay but that he, personally, had never experienced it. I said, "See you at the prayer tent at nine tonight!" He never showed up. I saw him later that evening and he explained that he had been called to a leaders meeting. Once again I said, "See you at the prayer tent the first thing in the morning". This time he showed up! As I prayed with him, he experienced the baptism of the Holy Spirit as manifested by resting in the Spirit. While he was resting in the arms of Christ, 10,000 men in the early morning session were singing, "Great is Thy Faithfulness". What a joyful experience, complete with goose bumps up my back!

Shortly after my first Promise Keepers event, six women of our local church surrounded me. They wanted to know about this new group that their husbands were becoming involved with. Mostly it was just inquisitiveness; however, a few women thought it was a macho type organization with anti-female leanings. I could sense that I was not going to win this debate. I simply suggested that these women speak to the wives of the other men who had attended the Promise Keepers event. Most of the men who attended this Promise Keepers event had a very positive experience and their wives were supportive. Many men developed a closer relationship with Christ through this organization.

Brothers in Christ

The 1996 Promise Keepers event at Soldiers Field in Chicago was such a powerful experience for many of us that we decided to form an early morning prayer ministry. We began at 6 a.m. on Wednesday mornings. Now many of you may be early morning people but I was not. I did not even know that 6 a.m. existed! Was the sun even up then? But I adjusted my wake up time, set the alarm clock for 5 a.m., found out the sun does rise by 6 and I began to attend.

Following our one-hour prayer time, we shared coffee and some breakfast snacks. Occasionally someone would bring special treats but usually just donuts and bagels. The half-hour afterglow was a great time of refreshment, discussion and fellowship. A majority of the men have to leave to catch a train or drive to work so the few retired men and local workers stay to clean up the kitchen. Our Brothers in Christ group has continued for over ten years and we regularly have 10 to 20 men attend the morning prayer meetings.

Aldersgate Renewal Ministries (ARM)

ARM is a network of United Methodists praying and working together for the spiritual renewal of the United Methodist Church, by the power of the Holy Spirit. The

ARM movement is committed to "Bringing the life of the Holy Spirit into the life of the Church" (www.aldersgate renewalministries.org). Since 1979, ARM has sponsored an annual national conference on the Holy Spirit, highlighting lively praise and worship while focusing on equipping believers for the work of the ministry. Besides this national Aldersgate Conference on the Holy Spirit for adults, youth and children, ARM has four team-led weekend renewal events.

+ Lay Witness Mission (LWM) encourages laypeople to tell of their experiences in their faith journey with God.
+ Lord Teach Us To Pray (LTUTP) encourages God's people to become a people of prayer.
+ Life In the Spirit Seminar (LISS) teaches participants how the Holy Spirit ministers in and through the life of the believer.
+ Worship In Spirit and Truth (WIST) is designed to equip participants with a biblical understanding of corporate and personal worship.

LISS, available in English and Spanish, is a life-changing weekend. Many of the experiences mentioned in this book have come from 19 weekend seminars, of which we have been privileged to be a part. Two of the Life in the Spirit weekends have been at Spanish speaking churches, even though we do not speak Spanish. Two other LISS events were in Brazil, where Portuguese is the language. Again, we do not speak Portuguese. Regardless of the language difference, the Holy Spirit can move through speaking in our heavenly language, commonly called speaking in tongues or letting the Spirit intercede for you. These weekend events are an excellent example of how laity can be involved in ministry of the church.

One day I was discussing ARM with a fellow believer and explained that Aldersgate Renewal Ministries is the charismatic arm of the United Methodist Church. He was surprised that I used the words charismatic and United Methodist in the same sentence. There is a very interesting document entitled "Guidelines: The United Methodist Church and The Charismatic Movement". Subsequent to its publication in 1976, this document was incorporated into the Book of Resolution of the United Methodist Church in 1996. In part that document states,

> *"Throughout this report, the term charismatic movement is used to identify the movement, which began about 1960 in mainline Christian bodies, both Protestant and Roman Catholic, reemphasizing the importance of the gifts of the Spirit in the life of the church. In a biblical sense, there is no such person as a "non-charismatic Christian" since the term charismata refers to the gracious gifts of God*

> *bestowed upon all Christians to equip them for ministry."*

Full Gospel Business Men Fellowship International, Promise Keepers, and Aldersgate Renewal Ministries are national organizations. More information about these organizations can be found on the web. The three other organizations, Project Understanding, Straight Talk and Brothers in Christ are primarily local groups. Local, national and international groups and movements are important to spreading the word of personal and corporate renewal. Personal spiritual growth can occur in many ways. My growth occurred through involvement in these organizations. These groups have helped to make me who I am.

What has contributed to make you who you are? Are you happy with who you are and the things that have contributed to your making? Remember, sometimes the answer finds you before you know the question.

CHAPTER 5 –
The Granville Blessing

"What is going on in the Northern Illinois Conference of the United Methodist Church with the Holy Spirit?"

That's how, in November 1997, I met Pastor John Hudson of the Granville Avenue United Methodist Church in Chicago. After we chatted for about 20 minutes, he arranged for me to visit his church's prayer and praise time on Wednesday evening. About 30 people met that evening and half stayed for an informal discussion time after the worship. John, his wife Susan, and many others in the church were very concerned about violence that was happening around their community. An 18-year-old African American boy had been murdered on the streets of Chicago by random gang violence. This was tearing their church apart. I suggested we have a word of prayer for his church. Now, often when I pray with others, the Spirit flows through me and rests on those I am touching. This was the case on that November evening.

I noticed John started to sway back and forth, so I got behind him and gently lowered him to the floor. We had discussed the phenomenon of "resting in the Spirit" earlier. So, I knew that he and Susan were familiar with this occurrence. Susan mentioned that she had seen this, but had never experienced it herself. She asked for prayer. Likewise, Susan "rested in the Spirit". Seven other people asked for prayer, four "rested in the Spirit" and three did not. However, they all received the infilling of the Holy Spirit, sometimes called the "Baptism of the Holy Spirit". It is not necessary to "rest" in order to be filled with the Holy Spirit, but it does have benefits. You will read more on this aspect later in this book.

While people were resting in the Spirit, an African American girl sat nearby, crying. One of the Granville men tried to counsel her but, to no avail. After finishing prayer with others, I went over to her, and likewise got nowhere. I asked her if she would like to have prayer. She was crying so hard that all she could do was to nod her head "yes". Because she came in on crutches and had her right leg and ankle bandaged, I asked her if she could stand. Again, she was just able to nod "yes". I took the anointing oil to anoint her. Before I could put the oil on her forehead, she was on the floor, resting in the Spirit. While she was on the floor, I prayed for the right leg, not knowing what the real problem was. Pastor John later reported that Katrina had walked out of the church that night without her crutches. Praise the Lord! Because of that evening's experiences, John has had a first-Friday-of-the-month revival since then, starting in March, 1998. It is now into its ninth year.

Testimony of Pastor John Hudson

A Testimony by Pastor John taken from the Granville UMC newsletter, The Messenger, dated November 15, 1997.

"The Granville Blessing"

"We pray for the Holy Spirit to come down on us, and it does, time and time again, in many ways. On November 5, I went down on the floor in the power of the Spirit. It was nothing weird. I floated down and was filled with light and well-being.

"I could hear what was going on around me, and was free in the Spirit. I was even more conscious than ever. It was a humbling experience in a positive sense. We really don't have control. God is in control.

"I noticed the floor was cold. I knew others were going down. It was time to return. I rejoice in a new happiness in the Lord.

"Those who went down reported a sense of well-being and light. They said they were strengthened in the faith.

"The 1990s are a special time with signs of the Spirit like this happening across the world. Our United Methodist Church started with revival signs in the 1700s. A study of revivals in this country and across the earth includes the outpouring of the

Gifts of the Spirit as described in the Bible. When the church cools down in passion, there is a move of God. At this time God invites us to be open and ready to claim the power of our faith! "

Susan Hudson also experienced the Holy Spirit that evening in November. She witnessed, "I used to be the world's worst worrier but since my 'rest', I haven't worried about anything."

Many great, peaceful benefits can come from resting in the Spirit.

Susan would like to share her testimony with you.

Testimony of Susan Hudson

Granville United Methodist Church
Dying To Ourselves

"It was the middle of the night on Labor Day weekend 1996, and my husband John and I were sound asleep when we were awakened by a great commotion. As we came down the stairs we heard that someone was shouting 'POLICE!' John, the pastor of Granville United Methodist Church, opened the door and in rushed one of our church members in a state of hysteria -- 'THEY'VE SHOT SOKARI! THEY'VE KILLED MY BABY!' Soon the horror of the situation became clear. One of the brightest, kindest, most accomplished young men ever to walk this planet was dead.

"He had just begun a new life as a student at the University of Illinois where he had received a full scholarship in engineering. Home for the weekend, he was the victim of random violence. Someone walked up to him and shot him in the neck, killing him instantly.

"The next week was a nightmare as everyone worked on the funeral arrangements. More than a thousand sobbing young people walked by his casket on the night of the wake. They were lined up for blocks outside the church, waiting to get in and pay final tribute to this fine young man. It was amazing how many friends he had! Because he had participated in the United Methodist Church camping program for many years, he was loved by people from all over northern Illinois.

"In the bleak months that followed this tragedy, it seemed like all hope was gone and that God had abandoned us. It certainly seemed clear that whatever we were doing as a church was not enough -- what were we really doing for our young people? What were we doing to change the lives of the kinds of people who threaten our children? What can we do to protect them? What did we offer Sokari? What can we offer the others?

"In the process of dealing with these challenges we did what most good United Methodists do - we set up programs. We began meeting every week to discuss what we could do to make our neighborhood a better place, to make things safer for the children. Eventually we ran out of steam.

"John's ministry had long centered on the need to heal racial and cultural divisions among God's people. His dream was to establish a multi-ethnic, inter-racial church. He had pastored at Granville for more than 20 years, and the church had begun to experience integration. Sokari's death and the resulting tensions exposed serious divisions between various groups starting to develop. And, Sokari's death brought out the worst in everyone. The white people felt that our worship was getting too "black" (too spirited), while the blacks were frustrated by the way the white people seemed to want to sit motionless and expressionless in their seats week after week. As for the Indians, Asians, Africans, and others -- who could tell what *they* really wanted! The level of frustration continued to build and church was becoming increasingly unpleasant. So many complaints! So many problems! We wondered if it were really possible to have a multi-ethnic church...maybe churches were inherently tied to and bound by the culture of the parishioners.

God Calls Our Church By Name

"The summer of 1997 was a turning point in our lives. We had an administrative council meeting and three people showed up. While I believed in my heart that white worship didn't have to be sober and expressionless, I had never experienced anything else. While on vacation we visited a very small Pentecostal church in South Haven, Michigan and the experience turned out to be a life-changing one.

"The worship was wonderful! For the first time I really felt at home in a church! People (--white people--) were actually praising God with all of their hearts! I was thrilled! They asked us to come back that evening for a special service, which we did. Again, the worship was great and the speaker was very good. Then, they gave an altar call and it seemed like "all heaven" broke loose. (Of course, having been raised a United Methodist, I didn't even really know what an altar call was. I wanted to go forward but wasn't sure if I'd be making some kind of mistake or joining their church or something). Some people began speaking in tongues (which didn't surprise me) and others began crying out as if in agony (which I'd never heard before). I myself was crying and I didn't know why, except that I was longing for God. They told us to turn around in our seats and kneel right where we were so John and I did this. At the same time, there was a sound that I couldn't identify. Above the music, and the tongues, and the crying, and the shouting there was another noise -- a sound like energy, a sound that had a tone that rose and fell, a sound unlike anything I had ever heard so I looked up and the place seemed to be filled with an awesome presence unlike anything I'd ever experienced.

"Eventually John and I left to go back to our motel. Usually when we leave a church we start chatting immediately - "What did you think of this or that?" "We should do such-and-such", etc. On this occasion neither one of us said a word for the longest time. Finally, I asked John, "Did you hear that noise?" He said, "That strange noise during the altar call?" Hmmm.... I knew something powerful had happened. Then a small voice crept into my thoughts, "I am the wind. I am the wind of Pentecost." And I told John, "It was God that made that noise" and as we pondered this, we became aware that our lives would never be the same, and neither would the church.

"So, what we learned was that if you really do what it says in the Bible – praise and worship the Lord with all of your heart - GOD WILL COME and reveal his physical presence!!! This was what church is supposed to be! This is what we've all been reaching for! Everything in the Bible is true! All of these thoughts ran through my mind, along with a deep sense of sorrow and repentance for all of the churches that had never experienced the manifest presence of God. I began to pray for change with all of my heart. I began to pray for the churches, especially the Methodist churches. I began to pray for our own congregation. I began to pray for myself and for more love in my heart. I now knew that God was present, but it seemed like we needed to do a lot of changing and cleaning up before we could have the kind of church that God would want to visit - the kind of church that was described in the book of Acts. Things still seemed a little hopeless.

"But God wanted us to change, so he gave us a lot of tools and a lot of help. During that same vacation in South Haven (and before visiting the church there), John felt drawn to a video from the Brownsville Assembly of God in Pensacola, Florida. When we got home, we put in this video and were thrilled to see thousands of people (--white people--) engaging in spirited worship. The particular video was also mystical and spiritual and you could feel the presence of God just by watching it! We showed it to others in the church and they were thrilled. Some of the black people were amazed to see white people jumping up and down in praise and worship! The video also showed us some intercessors praying, which touched our hearts. We knew that all things must begin in prayer -- Where were our intercessors?

The Holy Spirit Stirs Our Hearts

"We had been home only two weeks when John was approached by the principal of the local grade school, and said that she wanted to come to our Wednesday evening prayer. At the time, we only had 3 or 4 people coming, and the woman was a Pentecostal, so he told her that it was a small group, it wasn't really very spirited, and that she might not find it very satisfying. Her response -- "I can fix that!" The next Wednesday she came and prayed and we learned by her example. We prayed our hearts out to God that night, and then we invited others to come the next week and do the same. In another three weeks, our prayer group had swelled to more than 20 people, and on one night, we had thirty!

"Now that we were praying, things started changing. Our Sunday worship service was becoming more and more spirited, and we actually lost a few people who said that they couldn't handle the noise. The music was new - songs that had no cultural association with any group. After I testified to one of the young women in our congregation about our South Haven experience, she confessed that God had given her the gift of healing but she had not mentioned it because she was afraid we would be upset if she prayed in tongues. As a result of the testimony, she started praying for people and God started healing them - one man's shoulder was healed; another woman was healed of deep spiritual pain. We started praying more -- first immediately before the worship service, and then we added Saturday nights for cleansing the Sanctuary and preparing for worship.

God Shows Up At Granville

"When we first returned from South Haven, we also did some research and found out about the Aldersgate Renewal Ministries. John called Charlie Cilley, and he promised to visit our church. He seemed particularly interested in whether we had "rested in the Spirit". We didn't really understand what he was talking about, and it didn't really seem like anything we particularly needed. In November, I had arranged to give a testimony to the whole church about the South Haven experience. The Wednesday before I was scheduled to do this, Charlie visited our evening prayer group -- an event that changed our church forever!

"After the prayer was over there were about nine of us standing around talking, and John and I were talking to Charlie. He asked us about our church, and I was getting more and more upset. I talked about the children - one who was pregnant, one who had tried to commit suicide the week before, and of course Sokari. After hearing all of this, he asked us if we had ever rested in the spirit, and we said no. Suddenly he stood and said, "Let me pray for you." John and I got up and he put one of his arms around each of us and had just started to pray when John sort of slumped to the floor! I looked at him, kind of stunned. I couldn't believe that he had gone down like that. It seemed like he must have been faking it, but that would have been completely out of character. Charlie then turned to me, told me to hold out my hands like I was going to receive a gift, and he started to pray for me to be filled with the spirit. One part of me was praying to God, and another part was feeling sorry for Charlie because there was no way in the world that I was going to be falling on the floor. That was what I was thinking only a few seconds before I, myself, sort of floated to the floor.

"What a wonderful experience! I was down there for about a half an hour and I felt wave after wave of love, and peace, and the overwhelming presence of God. I was afraid to even move for fear that it would stop! I kept saying, "Thank you Lord" over and over again as I realized that He was so near!

"Meanwhile, while I was communing with God the other people in the room started to realize that something was happening on the other side of the room. Charlie moved around the room, praying for people, and each one was falling to the ground. One person had experienced this before, one had never heard of it. Most of us had heard of it but never figured that it was a real thing that would ever happen to us!

"In an act of profound courage (thank God!), my husband invited Charlie to come and preach at our church the next Sunday. In fact, he called every church member and exhorted them to come and experience the power and presence of God. Sure enough, God showed up during the service and many more people "fell under the power." At this point, we knew that our church would never be the same.

Chasing God.....

"Since then we have been working on planting a new church within the old. At the time that the Holy Spirit came, we averaged about 70 people a week. Today, we have about the same number - but almost all of the people are new. More than half were not associated with any church before they came to Granville. The gifts of the Spirit flow throughout the services. We have wonderful praise and worship. We are truly multicultural, and there are no divisions. We have a small but vibrant children's ministry. Our children know how to lay hands on people and pray for them. We have an excellent, interracial Gospel choir. We have monthly revivals, with guest speakers - many of who are UMC pastors. Everyone who visits our church agrees that something special is happening - which I believe could happen whenever a church that is fully integrated and fully charismatic. There are conversions, healings, and deliverance. There are extraordinary acts of kindness and generosity.

"My husband, myself, and many of the church members have become unabashed God Chasers. We have traveled all over the country seeking more of his presence and receiving prayer from many of God's anointed servants - John and Carol Arnott, John Kilpatrick, Benny Hinn, Che Ahn, Marvin Winans, Tommy Tenney, Margie Burger, and many others. We regularly attend other spirit-filled churches in the area. Whenever we travel, we go to as many churches as possible. Aldersgate has been a special blessing to us. We seek to remain a broken people that we might continue to receive the Lord. Although the church remains small, we believe that everything is going according to God's plan. We give thanks to the Lord for all he is doing, and we pray that all of the churches might surrender themselves to God and his life-giving Spirit!"

CHAPTER 6 –
Heavenly Inspiration

Alea Joy Kimmel, an artist, attended a "Wind and Fire Revival" during the summer of 2001 at the Des Plaines (Illinois) Methodist Camp Ground. As the result of her experience at that revival, Alea created three large paintings, which she has entitled "3rd Day Glory". The three 12' x 15' paintings were first hung in Waldorf Tabernacle at the Methodist Camp Ground in 2005. The Des Plaines Times newspaper printed an article entitled Heavenly Inspiration on August 4, 2005.

Alea Joy's personal explanation
of her experience is as follows
(personal communication, April 13, 2007)

"It was a hot day, and God surprised me again, a friend took me to a place in the woods. I had no idea where I was. It was a Tabernacle, built after the idea of the Eiffel Tower in Paris France, and still had a dirt floor, as it did when it was constructed in 1903. There was a revival going on there.

"During the winter of 2000, I had been in a near fatal accident in Mexico, up in the mountains, where I was doing missionary and artwork. I survived, but needed a lot of healing, so there I was.

"A preacher from Tennessee, whom I did not know, came from the far side of the tabernacle directly to me. He touched my forehead gently and said 'God has a word for you'. I went out under the power of the Holy Spirit and lay on the floor for two and half hours.

(Author's comment – many people have called this experience "slain in the Spirit", but I prefer to call it "resting in the Spirit". "Slain" is a harsh word, whereas "resting" denotes peace. When I have asked people who have had this experience what they felt, most people have indicated "peace", or a calmness or a restful feeling.)

"And, thus sayeth the Lord, '…this is the Experiential Gospel…I want the Black Arm and the White Arm of the Church to shake hands'… that was just a small part of it, there were many more words and visions, I received and heard from God, during this open and personal vision he gave me. The vision was all about His gospel going to the world, in the form of an International Multi-Media Art Event. Now, I am just like a small David, going after a Goliath… I have no idea, how in the world I will do what He told me to do. But God released his Holy Power and said also, that three is a very important number. I am to complete three paintings. He showed me the colors of each. They would be very large, with crosses and the story of each part of the gospel. So there I was, on the floor, questioning God, mind you. Why me? He said, I know you'll do it … ok? For the next month or so, I kept receiving messages wherever I went to church, to other events, crusades and revivals … while going out under the power again and again, until God was finished. The next part was up to me.

"What? Three paintings, approximately 15' x 20' each? I started praying and asking God, for practical answers. I did not have the money for the paints or the canvas and where was I going to do it? The Lord provided! The paint was donated by a wonderful Jewish man who owned a casket company. It took me awhile to understand what God was having me do and go through, to complete the vision. I just wanted to say 'Yes, Lord'. He said, the Joy of the Lord would be my strength, and In all thy ways,(ideas) acknowledge me, and I will direct your path. These are two great Scriptures to lean on.

> *"This day is sacred to our Lord. Do not grieve, for the joy of the Lord is your strength."* (Nehemiah 8: 10 NIV)

> *"Trust in the Lord with all your heart and lean not on your own understanding; in all your ways acknowledge Him and He will make your paths straight."* (Proverbs 3:5 – 6 NIV)

"It was a beautiful day and I felt a peace there, in the woods and a spiritual ecstasy … God was talking to me …that inner voice. I believed it.

"So, I went to a farm in Lena, Illinois and to a dear Methodist woman I had met there, Carole Fluegel. She took me in, paints and all, and lifted me up and down in a front-end loader. First, I was painting on the canvases on the side of the barn and then I went into a smaller manger area. I was surrounded by animals in the manger and I felt the presence of God there…all part of God's creation. I couldn't wait to wake up and hear the moos and the cockadoodle dos … all part of God's creation. I will tell you again, I did not paint them, God moved my hands and I was a vessel, only.

"The first painting is - Forgive me, Father … the second is Heal me, Lord and the third is I Love You, Lord.

"Forgive me, Father is black for Repentance, Salvation and Forgiveness.

"Heal me, Lord is Red for Healing, Deliverance and the Baptism of the Holy Spirit.

"I Love You, Lord is Gold, White and Blue for Celebration, Communion, Praise and Worship.

(I would add Resurrection to that list.)

"Come and sit before the Cross, come and stand, before me…As it is real to you…God will meet you where you are at and the church, the body of Christ, will be there for you…to lead you to the Lord, the path of the personal and experiential Gospel. That is what God wanted, to come to Him, Come to the Cross, personally.

"It had been three years, and then God resurrected the paintings and in one of His miracle stories, just like the old-time Bible stories, he brought them back from the farm in Lena Illinois on the top of a motor home to the Waldorf Tabernacle and from there the story took off. First, they were shown there at a Country Fair in August of 2005, on the stage, just as God said. Then they were exhibited at a youth rally and a family rally in the fall of 2006. The paintings are to go to all churches and denominations to further the work of the Kingdom of God and also help Israel.

"God made it clear that the Cross is not a denomination and it is to bring the white and black arm of the church together. Jews and Gentiles, whomever…and that the Gospel is Experiential…It is a beautiful realm to be in the heavenlies, to be brought back to life, and become a new creature."

Following is my description of these magnificent paintings, which truly are Heavenly Inspired.

Painting No. 1 - Hope For The Searcher

The predominantly-black background represents the darkness or the sins of the searchers. They have their hands extended at the foot of the cross, reaching up toward the rays of hope and the dove of the Holy Spirit flying at the top of the cross.

Painting No. 2 - Hope At The Cross

The red background symbolizes the blood of Christ, shed for <u>all people</u>, Those standing around in the distant background at the foot of the cross are symbolic of <u>all people</u>. The 39 lashes put on Christ's back are symbolized by the rays descending from above. The pool of blood at the foot of the cross stands for the redemption and purification of the believer. His blood makes all believers as white or as pure as snow.

Painting No. 3 - Hope For The Future

The third painting represents the hope for a believer's future, both on earth and in eternity. Because HE Lives, the Cross is empty, and we can face tomorrow. Because of Christ's resurrection the believer has assurance that the living Christ is always with them.

Hebrews 13:5b (NIV) states:

> *"… God has said: 'Never will I leave you; never will I forsake you'."*

This third painting reminded me of an experience that occurred during a Life In the Spirit Seminar held at Columbia, Illinois in the spring of 2001. During the Prayer Ministry time on Saturday night, David Pickering, came forward and requested an explanation of a vision that he had at his wife's recent funeral. David stated that during the funeral he had observed three angels hovering around the cross at the front of the church. He wanted to know what this meant. After asking the Lord for an interpretation, I stated, "They were God's angels coming to carry your wife home to heaven." This explanation was enough to break his mourning period. He then asked to receive the baptism of the Holy Spirit. For some reason he had not been able to tell his children about his vision. After resting in the Spirit, he was able to tell his two daughters about his vision. Each of his adult children and three friends, who had ministered to his wife during her illness, came forward and received the baptism of the Holy Spirit as manifested by resting in the Spirit.

It seems that visions and colors are quite common occurrences when one receives baptism of the Holy Spirit, as manifested by resting in the Spirit. Two additional stories exemplify this point.

At one Life In the Spirit Seminar a girl was sitting in the pew crying. When asked if she had a special prayer request, she couldn't respond. However, when asked if she would like to receive the baptism of the Holy Spirit, she shook her head, yes. After resting in the Spirit, she related this story. "When I was sitting on the pew I saw a hedge of green bushes closing in on me. While resting on the floor the hedge of bushes opened up and I saw Jesus standing there. It was at that point that my crying turned to joy."

She had a vision that comforted her!

At another Life In the Spirit Seminar in Georgia a woman came forward after the Sunday morning service to receive the baptism of the Holy Spirit. After receiving what the Lord had for her, she related seeing three different colors - black, red and yellow with a golden hue. I had three photos of Kimmel's paintings with me, which I showed her. So overcome by the colors in the photos, which were identical to those she had seen while resting, that she almost rested in the spirit again. God is truly amazing!

WHAT A COLORFUL GOD!!

CHAPTER 7 –
Healing of Backs

A Testimony of the Lord's Healing

A woman attending a Worship Conference at A.R.M. gave the following testimony.

"This is my second year coming to Aldersgate Renewal Ministry in Goodlettsville, Tennessee. I live in Southern California and I came to the conference alone. The Lord has been very faithful in my life. My church is really behind me and very supportive of this conference. During the Friday night prayer time, I answered God's call and went to the front of the hall. I felt the Lord tell me that my church back home really needed a revival. They are an obedient church but they need to surrender to the Lord. The Lord showed me that I needed to surrender also. The man praying for me had his hand on my head and he was praying for me. I don't remember what he was saying. The Holy Spirit was falling all over me -- a gentle pressure energy, not pushing, but just surrender. I had never been slain in the Spirit before. I was afraid, I was resisting, my toes were coming up in the air. I was afraid because I have a little bit of a bad back. It finally came over me that the Holy Spirit knows about my back so I just gave in. I was laid out on the floor and people were praying over me. The Lord was speaking to me about different things. After a while, I started to get up. As I was getting up I told the gentleman the reason I had resisted was that I was afraid of hurting my back. He said to lie back down and people prayed over my back. The man put my feet together and said he knows that people who have a bad back often have one leg shorter than the other. That was true in my case. He put my feet together and said they now are even. I just lay on the floor, accepting that. I just opened myself to receive whatever the Lord had for me. I had believed in physical healing but I had never experienced any physical healing. I had experienced emotional and spiritual healing but not physical healing. As I lay there, it was as if the Holy Spirit was pulling on my legs. I had what a chiropractor might call an adjustment. I had an adjustment as I lay on the floor. Normally there would be a big curve in my back because I had spinal curvature. I felt the Holy Spirit relaxing my spine and straightening it out. When I went home to the hotel, I was afraid to look in the mirror. But I did. My back was so much straighter than it had been for years and has remained that way. I pray that the Lord will continue to straighten me out and straighten all of us out. I want to give God the glory because he gives us what we need even when we don't ask."

In complete surrender, we come closer to the Lord. When we come into the presence of God we cannot stand, hence we rest in the Spirit, in the ever-loving arms of Jesus. This woman experienced this resting and was healed. Imagine what God will do for you!

In a jovial manner the leader of the worship conference said, "I just wonder, is it okay to get healed at a worship conference? That wasn't in the agenda."

The woman who gave the above testimony interrupted to say, "The first night we were here I was so blessed. Charlie, I never met you before but when you brought the streamer (banner) down, I knew it was going to be a good time. You're never too old to serve the Lord or praise the Lord or worship the Lord. It was such a blessing to my heart. I thank you and I knew it was going to be good from that moment."

The leader jokingly said that actually he is only 24 years old but just looks older. Remember that one of the points in the preface to this book is that one is never too young or too old to serve in the Lord's kingdom.

There will be more about banners in volume 2 of *Who Needs A Comforter*. For now, I believe it is sufficient to say, when I wave a banner, I tell people it is in accordance with the following scripture in the Bible:

> *"He has taken me to the banquet hall, and his banner over me is love." (Song of Songs 2: 4 NIV)*

When I wave the banner over people, I tell them that God's love is over them.

The Holy Spirit helps us in many ways. Sometimes we experience unexpected healing. A Korean pastor received such a gift of healing. After viewing the video tapes from the Toronto Airport Blessing and Brownsville Experiences, we discussed the Holy Spirit. The Korean pastor had felt the nudge of the Holy Spirit and asked for the baptism. When he received the Holy Spirit, as manifested by resting in the Spirit, I noticed one leg was longer than the other. I asked the Lord to grow the shorter leg out to equal the length of the other. The Lord is faithful! When the pastor sat up, I asked him how long he had had back trouble. He had been in an automobile accident about two years ago and had not been able to sleep on his back since that time. He had been "resting in the Spirit" for more than 20 minutes and the entire time he was on his back. He couldn't believe it! But something else confused him. He asked how I knew that he had back trouble. My response was that because his legs were different length I knew he undoubtedly had back trouble. When he stood up, his back pain was gone.

Praise the Lord for healed backs!

The phone rang interrupting my writing. A gentleman from Reading, Pennsylvania, called to give me an update on God's work in his life. Marj and I had experienced his and his wife's hospitality during a Life In The Spirit Seminar in 2004. They had welcomed us into their home for the weekend.

During the seminar's prayer ministry time on Saturday night, he had received the baptism of the Holy Spirit, as manifested by resting in the Spirit. For years, he had experienced back pain and reoccurring back problems. He reported that after his experience of resting in the Spirit, he was healed!

Praise God for healed backs!

Our conversation by phone continued. He mentioned that he had changed churches and on April 2, 2006 was ordained as a minister in his church. He's not sure what the Lord has in store for him but something is brewing. His church has approximately 100 acres of property in Dominican Republic. They plan to develop it into a complex consisting of an orphanage, a church, a parsonage and other buildings to serve the Lord. This will certainly assist in the advancement of the kingdom of God in the Dominican Republic.

This phone call came at an interesting time. Why was he led to call at this time? He related that they had been thinking of us every month or two since 2004 but had misplaced our phone number. Just recently, they had moved the bed in the room where Marj and I had stayed and found our telephone number on a slip of paper. This appears to be another mystery of life. He found our number just when I was writing this chapter. His testimony and telephone call demonstrates how the Lord watches over us all.

CHAPTER 8 –
Sleeping Disorder

Sleep. We all need it. Our bodies recharge for the busy day ahead. But what happens when sleep eludes you? Have you ever had trouble sleeping?

One Saturday morning a seminar team member came in looking like she had been dragged "through a knothole". She related that she had not slept well the night before. Actually, she confessed it was more than just the last night; she had difficulty sleeping many nights.

We prayed that she would have the peace of Christ and receive the infilling of the Holy Spirit. On Sunday morning during testimony time, she witnessed to the power and the presence of the Holy Spirit that gave her strength to continue on through Saturday. She also related how she had slept much better Saturday night than she had for several months.

> *"May the God of hope fill you with all joy and peace as you trust in Him, so that you may overflow with hope by the power of the Holy Spirit."* (Romans 15:13 NIV)

Eric Schlatterer had trouble sleeping, too. He had not been able to sleep well lately. During a prayer meeting, he commented about his sleeping problem. I commented, "A touch from the Lord would be in order". A comment from one of the group was: "That sounds like the best altar call ever". When the prayer meeting ended, Eric approached me and asked for prayer.

I asked Eric if he had any idea why he was having trouble sleeping. He did not. We reviewed Acts 1:4-5 and prayed that he would be filled with the Holy Spirit after he released his "Jerusalem" to the Lord.

> *"On one occasion, while He was eating with them, He gave them this command: 'Do not leave Jerusalem, but wait for the gift my Father promised, which you have heard Me speak about. For John baptized with water, but in a few days you will be baptized with the Holy Spirit.' "* *(Acts 1: 4-5 NIV)*

Lo and behold, when he had completely turned his "Jerusalem" over to the Lord, he received the infilling of the Holy Spirit, as manifested by resting in the Spirit. I told him that I believed he had been burdened with the issues that caused this sleeping problem for 20 years or more. He replied that it had been 20+ years. Eric now sleeps soundly again.

Praise the Lord!
Praise the Lord for release!

Ever since that day, Eric always has a smile and a friendly greeting. His wife has even noticed the difference in him. Since that Monday night, she has been delighted with her "new" husband.

But, God Wasn't Finished With Eric Yet.

Eric has told his story in the following testimony:

"I felt a great deal of spiritual relief after resting in the Spirit and I slept better than I had in a long time. But after resting in the Spirit, I was still experiencing a great deal of anxiety. The smile you saw on my face after that prayer session was a Spirit given determination not to let the enemy get the better of me. Finally, after about three months with no additional improvement in my anxiety, I came back to Charlie and asked for prayer. It was after resting in the Spirit a SECOND time that the Lord revealed to me that there was also a physical component to my anxiety. An adjustment to my diet brought me the additional relief I was seeking. The smile that you saw on my face after resting in the Spirit this second time reflected the peace and calmness stated in Romans 15:13".

> *"May the God of hope fill you with all joy and peace as you trust in Him, so that you may overflow with hope by the power of the Holy Spirit." (Romans 15: 13 NIV)*

Eric continues in his testimony:

"In summary, the Lord used this sleeping disorder to bring me onto His straight and narrow path once and for all. I had been "saved" for almost 6 years but hadn't truly begun my walk with Him until this onset. My life has been unalterably and delightfully changed ever since. I now look forward to the remainder of my journey in this life with great expectation."

I believe there is a direct correlation between having the peace of Christ in your heart and being able to sleep soundly. The majority of the people who receive the infilling of the Holy Spirit, as manifested by resting in the Spirit, experience a peace that they have never had before.

A passage from Corrie Ten Boom's book, *Each New Day*, seems to hit the nail on the head.

> *"When I was a little girl, my father used to tuck me into bed at night. He talked with me, prayed with me, and laid his big hand on my little face. I did not move because I wanted to keep the feeling of that big hand on my face. It was a comfort to me.*
>
> *"Later, when I was in the concentration camp, I would sometimes pray, 'My heavenly Father, will you lay Your hand on my face?' That would bring me peace, and I would be able to sleep." (p.114)*

There are many ways to receive the peace of Christ; being filled with the Holy Spirit is just one of them.

Jesus said:

> *"All this I have spoken while still with you. But the Counselor, the Holy Spirit, whom the Father will send in my name, will teach you all things and will remind you of everything I have said to you.*
>
> *Peace I leave with you; my peace I give to you. I do not give to you as the world gives. Do not let your hearts be troubled and do not be afraid."* (John 14:25-27 NIV)

CHAPTER 9 –
Why Do You Push?

Whenever this question comes up, I always think back to a Saturday morning at a National Aldersgate Holy Spirit conference. Two 14-year-old boys confronted me with the question, "Why do you push people when you pray with them?" They had seen what appeared to them, as people being pushed to the floor.

I always appreciate it when people ask questions that are on their minds. It gives me an opportunity to explain or at least share my beliefs. Many times situations appear to become exaggerated when the observer does not understand what is happening.

Their question gave me the opportunity to explain what I believe happens when one rests in the Spirit. I believe when one comes into the presence of Christ it is not possible to stand. The Bible tells us that when Paul was on the road to Damascus a light from heaven came around him and he fell to the ground.

> *"As he neared Damascus on his journey, suddenly a light from heaven flashed around him. He fell to the ground and heard a voice say to him, 'Saul, Saul, why do you persecute me?'"* (Acts 9:3 – 4 NIV).

Another example is when the soldiers came to arrest Jesus in the Garden of Gethsemane and they fell to the ground when they realized who He was. In the 18th chapter of John we find,

> *"Jesus knowing all that was going to happen to him, went out and asked them, 'Who is it you want?' 'Jesus of Nazareth.' they replied. 'I am he,' Jesus said. (And Judas the traitor was standing there with them.)" When Jesus said, 'I am he,' they drew back and fell to the ground."* (John 18: 4- 6 NIV)

I have often wondered whether they fell forward or backwards. Most people when they have this experience fall backwards. However, I've had several people fall forward. Because of this possibility, I always pray with my eyes open. If someone begins to fall forward I am aware and can catch them. Otherwise, they would fall into me and I would go down also.

To receive the fullness of God's blessings, we must completely surrender ourselves to Christ. When we come into His presence as a result of the baptism of the Holy Spirit, we can then rest in the Spirit.

After explaining to the boys why it appears that people are pushed and explaining what happens when one receives the baptism of the Holy Spirit, as manifested by resting in the Spirit, I asked the boys if they would like to receive the gift of the Father.

> *"On one occasion, while He was eating with them, He gave them this command: 'Do not leave Jerusalem, but wait for the gift my Father promised, which you have heard Me speak about.'"* *(Acts 1: 4 NIV)*

Both of the boys excitedly agreed to have prayer. We went to the carpeted prayer ministry area at the front of the meeting hall. I prayed for the boys to be filled with the Holy Spirit. As the Holy Spirit filled them, they fell to the floor and rested in the Spirit. When they stood up, I asked them if they felt as if they had been pushed. They said they had not! A year later during a phone conversation, the boys both reported that school had become easier and their grades had improved. They attributed this to their new relationship with God the Father, Jesus the Son, and the Holy Spirit.

No matter what your situation is, I believe, that if you release your burdens and are subsequently filled or baptized of the Holy Spirit, remarkable things can and often do happen. Many people have witnessed that their attitude and outlook on life have greatly improved after resting in the Spirit.

A well-known Bible teacher and conference speaker has also experienced being accused of pushing when praying with people. Both of us have said, "I don't mean to push. If I did, I am sorry for that. However, when the Spirit of God comes through you, it is possible to get a little too rambunctious."

When you receive the infilling of the Holy Spirit, it is the power of God that pushes you down.

When people do not discuss their concerns, the ways of the Lord cannot be discussed or explained. If you ever have questions, ask. Only then can you fully understand. Usually, the Holy Spirit answers most of your questions, if you allow Him to come into your heart and be active in your life.

To Understand Is To Know

It is very important to explain the manifestations that might occur during prayer ministry. One of our local churches held a Saturday evening contemporary service and several people rested in the Spirit during the prayer ministry time. No one had taken time during the service to explain this phenomenon, so people were caught off guard. This was the first and only Saturday evening contemporary service held at that church. We were sad that this type of contemporary service was not continued. A short time later, a new pastor arrived at the church. She asked about the contemporary service and heard from several people that everything was fine until the "fainting started". Obviously, they were not familiar with or did not understand resting in the Spirit. When people have knowledge of the Spirit, they are less afraid. When they know that resting in the Spirit is a blessing, they possess the words to express their experience properly. People become more accepting when knowledge exists.

My experience has been that if someone does not understand or criticizes resting in the Spirit, he or she has undoubtedly never experienced it. When I've asked people if they have received the baptism of the Holy Spirit, as manifested by resting in the Spirit, quite often they answer, I think I have, I believe I have, or I hope I have. When I hear these answers, I believe the person has not received the fullness of the Holy Spirit as God intended. Most people KNOW after receiving the baptism of the Holy Spirit, as manifested by resting in the Spirit, that they have been baptized with the Holy Spirit! They do not have to think or question whether they have or have not; they KNOW for sure that they have received the Spirit with all it's blessings and power!

Laying On Of Hands

Some people have said that it is not necessary to touch the person in order to have them rest in the Spirit. One organization suggests that people do not need to be touched while being prayed for. They suggest only that a hand is waved over and around the person. If God wants to touch an individual, He does not need physical hands to do that. However, I believe there are benefits to actually laying on of hands.

First, laying on of hands is biblical.

> *"He could not do any miracles there, except lay His hands on a few sick people and heal them."* (Mark 6:5 NIV)

> *"Once more Jesus put His hands on the man's eyes. Then his eyes were opened, his sight restored, and he saw everything clearly."* (Mark 8:25 NIV)

> *"....Paul went in to see him and, after prayer, placed his hands on him and healed him."* (Acts 28:8b NIV).

Paul also explained how early Christians received the Holy Spirit.

> *"When the apostles in Jerusalem heard that Samaria had accepted the word of God, they sent Peter and John to them. When they arrived, they prayed for them that they might receive the Holy Spirit, because the Holy Spirit had not yet come upon any of them; they had simply been baptized into the name of the Lord Jesus. Then Peter and John place their*

hands on them and they received the Holy Spirit."
(Acts 8:14 -17 NIV)

Paul explained that the Samaritans had received the water baptism but had not received the Holy Spirit baptism. Could this be what John meant in John 3: 5?

> *"Jesus answered, 'I tell you the truth, no one can enter the kingdom of God unless he is born of water and the Spirit.'" (John 3: 5 NIV)*

Jesus also explained,

> *"For John baptized with water, but in a few days you will be baptized with the Holy Spirit." (Acts 1:5 NIV)*

To me it is very clear that the baptism of the Holy Spirit may be a second blessing beyond salvation and water baptism.

Before laying on of hands, one should ask permission to do so. If permission is not given, do not lay on hands. When the person I am praying for is receiving, my hand gets warm, sometimes even hot. If the person I am praying for is not receiving or has a self imposed barrier, my hand will stay a normal temperature or even get cool. I realize this may not occur for everyone who does prayer ministry but it has been my personal experience. The sense of temperature has been very beneficial to me during prayer ministry.

A word of caution to those involved with prayer ministry. During my earlier days of prayer ministry, I would allow my hand to follow people to the floor as they rested in the Spirit. This action gave the observer, the person sitting in the pew, or the skeptic, the appearance of pushing. I have since stopped doing that and now I simply lightly touch the person on the forehead when anointing with oil.

One should also ask permission to anoint with oil, especially if using a perfumed variety of anointing oil. Some people are allergic to perfume while others may experience a red mark on their forehead. Personally, I prefer using the unscented anointing oil. If you wish to make the biblical anointing oil, the following verses give instructions.

> *"Take the following fine spices: 500 shekels of liquid myrrh, half as much (that is, 250 shekels) of fragrant cinnamon, 250 shekels of fragrant cane, 500 shekels of cassia- all according to the sanctuary shekel- and a hin of olive oil. Make these into a sacred anointing oil, a fragrant blend, the work of a perfumer. It will be the sacred anointing oil."*
> *(Exodus 30: 23- 25 NIV)*

Resisting The Spirit

Self imposed barriers and resistance to the Spirit, are touchy subjects. I have been criticized for asking someone whom I sense is not receiving from the Lord, why they are resisting the move of God. I realize that many people think it is not politically correct or good practice to be straightforward and direct about the experience of the Holy Spirit. However, it has been extremely meaningful to me to be forthright in asking. If someone is receiving the Spirit but resisting to rest in the Spirit, there is usually a reason.

I have heard answers like: I am not worthy, I have had broken bones, I am afraid of falling, I don't know, I have curvature of the spine, I was pushed down before, I don't want to look foolish, and I've experienced that before and I don't need it again. I think these are all good excuses and barriers to receiving everything the Lord has for you. If we will surrender completely all our cares, worries, excuses, barriers, shame, guilt, resentment, anger, depression and control to the Lord, He can then come in with all of His blessings that He has for you at that time. If you continue to hold on to any of these factors, you are resisting the move of the Lord. As you read this list, many other thoughts and ideas may come into your mind. Let God be in control!

At one of the Life In the Spirit Seminars, two couples came up to me on Sunday morning after the worship service and asked to receive prayer for the baptism of the Holy Spirit. However, one partner of each couple said they were not going to fall down. I indicated to them I would be glad to pray for them but it was not up to them or me whether they would fall to the floor. I believe that is God's business. When I prayed for them, all four people rested in the Spirit.

Trying to tell the Lord how, when and where you are going to receive His blessings, especially the baptism of the Holy Spirit, is basically saying that you are still in control or you have a hidden burden. This could be what I mean as your Jerusalem that has not been released to Jesus. Complete surrender and release of your burden is mandatory before you can have a more complete relationship with Jesus Christ. I don't mean to say that God's will is for everyone to rest in the Spirit. I know Jesus can baptize a person any way He wishes and will not always baptize in the same manner. But I believe a positive attitude of expectation is important when entering into prayer time.

A woman in Arizona called my wife and me to come pray for her healing. When we got to her house, she started telling us, and God, *how* she was going to be healed. Obviously, nothing happened when we prayed for her healing. It is important to get out of the way and let God be in charge. Do you not agree that God knows better what we need than we do ourselves? That is why we can go to Him when we cannot put our needs into words. He will tell us or refresh our memory! God is an awesome God!

Recently while praying with a woman, I felt she was resisting and not receiving the gift of God the Father. When asked why, she said she was afraid of falling because she had broken many bones. God lets no harm come to those truly under the power of the Holy Spirit. She let go and let God in. She was not hurt. Praise be to God!

Many people have retold experiences of being in God's loving hands. The woman in a car accident told of flying through the windshield and floating to the ground in God's loving embrace. The young man who rested in the Spirit in a small living room had God's loving hands surrounding him. His mother felt no pain as she slammed into a coffee table as she bore his weight. God had cushioned her fall. There was a man who hit his head on the front pew when he rested in the Spirit. The impact made such a sound that his wife came running over thinking that he had been hurt. He had no repercussions from hitting his head nor hardly remembered hitting the pew. God protects those in His love.

Who Will Catch?

It is very important to have trained catchers to graciously let someone down to the floor when they receive the baptism of the Holy Spirit, as manifested by resting in the Spirit. Some people fall gently, others crumble, and still others topple like a giant Redwood. The catcher must be prepared for every occurrence. A courtesy cloth should also be placed over those who are resting, especially women. This is a hemmed piece of cloth approximately four feet square. These cloths serve as a comfort and a cover for those resting in the Spirit. While there is no biblical reference for courtesy cloths, that I know of, it is a comfort to many to be covered.

How Long Do You Stay Mad?

Many times due to my direct and frank statements about the Spirit, people become upset or even angry. During another Life In The Spirit Seminar, I heard that I had made someone mad. A person related to me that the year before I had said that I believed they did not have the Holy Spirit in their heart. This person was mad because they disagreed with my statement.

Now some people stay mad for hours, some for days, and some stay mad for years. However, when we release our anger and let God in, wonderful things happen.

How long had this person stayed mad? Fifteen minutes and then the Holy Spirit came upon them. This person then understood why I felt they had not experienced it before. However, the anger, at that time, was so powerful, that it was remembered for the entire year and remembered to tell me about it.

As I will mention later, many people hold such anger, abuses, guilt and shame for a long time. Possibly for a lifetime in some cases. The only way to be free from such conditions and anxiety is to cast your cares upon the Lord.

CHAPTER 10 –
Thank You, Lord!

When we receive a gift from a friend or relative, we usually send a thank you note or acknowledge the gift in some way. It is the same when we receive a blessing or a gift from our heavenly Father. His blessings to us, answers to our prayers, and His grace and mercy are all a few of His gifts to us. We should say Thank You Lord for His gifts.

> *"Always giving thanks to God the Father for everything, in the name of our Lord Jesus Christ."* (Ephesians 5:20 NIV)

Jessica

Getting e-mails from our children is nothing unusual but in January 2006, we received a special one from our daughter, Paula. She informed us that her daughter, Jessica was accepted into the Sports Medicine Program at the University of Illinois. This is an elite program and less than half of the students that applied were accepted. Jessica was ecstatic to be part of this program. It would certainly enhance her study of Occupational and Physical Therapy.

When I first read the e-mail I said, "Thank You, Lord". This may sound strange. Why would someone thank the Lord for such a life event? God's plans are not always our plans. If fact, they seldom are. However, we can thank the Lord for His plans and their eventual goodness. If we knew what God's plan was, we would probably try to change it. You see, we like to be in control. God had a plan for Jessica and me. My experiences became the basis for her opportunities. Throughout the following experience, I was definitely *not* in control. Could I, or even *should* I, say "Thank You, Lord"?

The Experience

In July 2005, I had a mishap that caused a six-month delay in my plans. Was it God's plan? I attended a concert at the DesPlaines Methodist Campground featuring the musical group, The Mad Monks of Melody. They played Dixieland jazz religious music and ended their program with *"When the Saints Go Marching In"*. This song always gets my feet tapping and my hands clapping. I wanted to parade around. So, I did! Soon there were 50 to 75 people parading behind me. What a great time of praising and worshiping the Lord! Worship can be an exciting joyful time! Well, I got over-exuberant, lost my balance and put down my cane to steady myself. My old wooden cane broke and I fell to the ground. It didn't take long to know I had a broken wrist.

Could I say, Thank you, Lord? Not yet!

We had eight guests at the concert and we had planned to have ice cream at our cottage after the concert. I tried to convince them to enjoy the ice cream but everyone wanted me to get to the hospital. The pain was not too great and much to my disappointment, no one would stay for ice cream. That night started another venture in my life that has encouraged me to keep my eyes on Jesus.

Thank you, Lord? Maybe.

The emergency room visit gave me an opportunity to pray with the physician's assistant. The visits with the doctor and pre-surgical nurses provided me many opportunities to praise the Lord again through the story of how my accident happened. Before my surgery in August, I was able to pray with the doctor.

Thank you, Lord? We're getting there.

During surgery, they installed a fixator on my right arm due to the severe compression fracture. After many weeks the final x-rays showed that the bone had healed better than normal. The spot of fracture is now hardly visible to my untrained eye. However, it was necessary to have occupational therapy. So began four months of intense therapy at the Des Plaines facility of the Illinois Bone and Joint Institute.

Thank you, Lord? Almost.

During this time, I heard that Jessica was interested in occupational and physical therapy. I thought it would be a good experience for her to visit the Des Plaines facility and see what she was getting into. After checking with Julee Brennan, the manager of the occupational therapy section, it was arranged. Jessica visited for two days during her Christmas break from college. Getting to actually see the work that occupational and physical therapists do was extremely beneficial for Jessica. I believe this experience helped her when she applied for the Sports Medicine Therapy program. Her big acceptance interview took place just three days after her return to school after Christmas break.

Thank you, Lord? Certainly!

Many people could say that this was a matter of coincidence and that it all just fell together. But, I do not believe there are such things as *coincidences*. I believe they are *God incidences*. In other words, God is in control. The accident, the surgery, the four month rehabilitation, meeting new friends at rehab, and Jessica being accepted into the Sports Medicine program are all part of God's plan for me. God's plan – definitely not my plan.

THANK YOU, LORD!!

Brian

Aldersgate Renewal Ministries (ARM) has been a major part of my life for the past eight years. Brian Reynolds, our grandson, attended the Holy Spirit Conference of the United Methodist Church for the first time in 2005. He was very apprehensive about going but ventured off to Overland Park, Kansas with my wife, Marj, and I.

Brian had many reasons for his apprehension. He had just graduated from college and felt God calling him into ministry. He had spent several summers in the Czech Republic as part of group working with children at an English Camp sponsored by his church and he felt called to return to the churches in Valtice and Mikolov. Brian's plans included teaching English and working with the youth. But, was this God's plan? Did He really want Brian to travel 8000 miles from home to a country where few people even spoke English?

Yes, Brian was apprehensive! When the conference started, he went off to the Young Adult group. It was a friendly welcoming group. A woman walked up to him and said, "Hi, Brian, I'm Catharine. I have a word for you from the Lord. The Father says, 'What you are planning to do is in my plan for your life. Just continue on with your plans and I will be with you, all the way.'"

Brian had received his affirmation. He *was* walking with God!

Thank you, Lord!

God works in mysterious ways. Brian had never met Catharine before their conversation nor did he remember her full name. He just knew that God had sent someone to him to calm his worries. I shared my grandson's story the following year at The Gathering of ARM in March, 2006. Catharine explained to me that she was the one who had received the words and shared them with Brian. Praise the Lord for people like Catharine Cwanek who are responsive to what the Lord is saying to them and willing to speak up.

THANK YOU, LORD! !

Catharine's Daughter- Torilinn

When I walked into The Gathering in March 2006, they were in the midst of worship. During ARM worship services, it is normal for me to wave a banner. {My banner is approximately 3-4 inches wide, and four feet long. Three different colors of cloth sown into one long strip are attached to a wooden dowel with a swivel hook so the banner does not wrap around the dowel when it is waved. It reminds me of the Father, Son & Holy Spirit.

As I gently or vigorously wave the banner it reminds me of the ways that God moves over and around us. Sometimes He is gentle, like a calm day in the spring. Sometimes He is vigorous, like a tornado or a tsunami. It is God's love, through the Holy Spirit, floating over ALL people - both His people who have accepted Jesus Christ as their Lord & Savior and His children, who have not as yet accepted Jesus Christ as their Lord and Savior. Because God created ALL of us HE loves ALL of us! }

> *"He has taken me to the banquet hall, and His banner over me is love." (Song of Songs 2: 4 NIV)*

Catharine Cwanek's mother, Sally, brought her granddaughter up to me and said, "I have someone who wants to meet you. She saw you waving the banner and would like to wave it too." I gave her my banner and made a friend for the rest of The Gathering.

During the testimony time on Sunday morning, this little girl took my hand and we walked to the front of the worship center. We gave our testimony to God, by her presence and not her words, that we are not too young or too old to worship God together. What a joy and a comfort to have this lovely and vivacious little girl as a new found friend. We really are never too young or too old to be a comfort to others. We all need a Comforter!

THANK YOU, LORD! !

Canaan In The Desert

Canaan in the Desert in Phoenix, Arizona is advertised as a 'Garden of Jesus' Suffering and Resurrection'. The Evangelical Sisterhood of Mary in the USA sponsors it. Basilea Schlink, now called Mother Basilea, founded this religious order in 1947 in postwar Germany.

> *"In the sixties, when Mother Basilea saw waves of lawlessness rolling in and covering our countries, she wrote:*
>
> *'In these dark, godless times of ours, centers and homes are needed that manifest God's kingdom of love. And a joy-filled life stemming from repentance is the key to this kingdom of love.'*
>
> *At that time God called Canaan in the Desert into being." (Used by permission of Canaan In The Desert. Permission granted by Sr. Rebekka Fraenkel. All rights reserved.)*

Marj and I visited this beautiful place in 2006. We were blessed to be a part of a special tour with the "Mature Group" of Mission Bell United Methodist Church of Glendale, Arizona. This group has monthly meetings and they tour points of interest, such as Canaan in the Desert, in the surrounding countryside. Since the Mature Group consists mostly of retired people they hold these functions in the morning, followed by luncheon at a local restaurant. This type of activity and fellowship is an excellent way to bring people of churches or a community together.

Many people have shared their thoughts about this place. Some have said:

"Just driving onto your property brings a sense of peace and rest over one's soul." And someone observed:

"Our group visited your Garden and Chapel. It was such a calming and healing experience that we all vowed to visit again with other friends." Another person shared:

"The Garden is my safe haven and I thank God that He gave me this little piece of heaven."

What a serene lovely spot in God's creation to reflect on Christ's suffering, death and glorious resurrection - any time of the year.

Sr. Bliss led our group on a tour of 'My Walk through the Prayer Garden'. We were blessed by Sr. Bliss' natural, sincere, thorough, and loving attitude. I was so impressed by her loving and tender comments that she made me think of Mary, the mother of Jesus. It was indeed a blessing to be with Sr. Bliss. These words of Mother Basilea, printed on a plaque at the Gethsemane station in the Prayer Garden hold a special meaning to me-

"My Father, I Do Not Understand You, But I Trust You!"

Many times I've asked, Why me Lord? I haven't *understood* why the Lord would ask me, a layman and an unknown, to write such an important book as this one. I have had to say many times throughout this endeavor,

> "You, dear children, are from God and have overcome them, because the one who is in you is greater than the one who is in the world." (I John 4: 4 NIV)

I believe this verse means "the one", who is in me is God the Father, God the Son and God the Holy Spirit. "The one" who is in the world is the prince of this world, none other than Satan.

Yes, it is true, I do not always understand what God is doing or saying about all of the mysteries of life. However, I *do* believe and trust in Him and attempt to follow His leading, guidance and direction.

Canaan in the Desert offers visitors meaningful, reflective and meditative spots to commune with our Heavenly Father. Although my poor memory is a topic of many family discussions, I remember other peaceful meditative places. The Bok Tower Gardens in Florida, The Thorncrown Chapel in the Ozark Mountains, and the Chapel of the Holy Cross in Sedona, Arizona, all bring fond memories. I am grateful for these memories, for these beautiful meditative spots, and for every place of peace throughout the world. For all of these, I say,

THANK YOU, LORD! !

Matthew

What does it take to take to stand true to God? How do you stand up to the pressures of a non-believing society? Our grandson, Matthew, took a stand after attending the Aldersgate Holy Spirit Conference in 2004. As a sophomore in high school, he started a Bible study that met in the library of his public school. The group started small but gradually grew to more than 10 kids. Imagine a Bible Study group in a public school!

THANK YOU, LORD ! !

After Matthew's second year at Aldersgate Holy Spirit Conference, 2005, he felt the call to become a chaplain in the U.S. Army National Guard. He completed boot camp at Fort Jackson, South Carolina during the summer of 2006 between his junior and senior year in high school. In a phone call home during the first week of basic, he reported how extremely difficult it was mainly because of all the swearing and coarse jokes that were being told. The recruits gave each other nicknames and after finding out that Matthew was planning to be a chaplain, they nicknamed him "Chap". After a particularly rough day, Matthew prayed for strength and peace. He felt he couldn't survive an entire summer of this. The next day one of the soldiers said to the group of recruits that he was fed up with all the swearing and crude jokes and he was sure it was bothering Chap, too. Their language improved. Two of the recruits even asked Matthew to pray with them.

Sometimes it takes conflict and hardship to help us grow. Throughout it all and because of it all, we can continue to say:

THANK YOU, LORD ! !

Answered Prayers - Ruth

"Army Basic Training is a tough experience for anyone but it was especially challenging for our 17 year-old son. Matthew answered God's call to be a chaplain assistant with the National Guard and began his training during the summer between his junior and senior year of high school. Away from home for the first time and halfway across the country, Matthew truly needed comfort. Would God provide a comforter for him? It is amazing how God comforts us and guides our thoughts and actions to connect us to each other.

"One morning as I walked through our neighborhood, I found myself by the Kankakee River. I cherish this quiet time of day filled with devotion and reflection. I knew that Matthew was completing a three-day field exercise and he had written that he was fearful of the physical and emotional challenges of the exercise. As I walked along the river, I had an overwhelming feeling. Matthew needed my help! As I prayed I heard, 'Carry Matthew's load'.

"Um, this was unusual. Was God telling me to help Matthew? I continued to walk along the river and tried to reason this out. Logic is a strong friend of mine!

"Carry Mathew's load. What was going on? I kept walking and thinking, thinking and walking. This does not make sense -- could God be talking to me? Could God be telling me that Matthew needs help? I kept hearing, 'Carry Matthew's load'.

"Finally, I gave in. Logic gave up and God won. I prayed for our dear son 800 miles from home. 'Matthew, I think you need some help. Let me carry your load... Let me help you carry your load'.

"Only vaguely aware of the passing minutes, the trees along the river, and the steadily increasing incline of the terrain, I prayed. 'Matthew, let me carry your load. Let me *help you* carry your load'.

"Minutes dragged on. My hike continued. I found myself deep in the woods on a well -- worn path headed home.

"Could it be? Are prayers really answered? Does God <u>really</u> hear us in this busy crazy world?

"My back began to sweat. Pressure increased on my shoulders. My legs grew weary. The hill became more difficult to climb. The weight of Matthew's pack became real! I even glanced around to see if perhaps the pack had appeared on my back. Nothing was there! Never had a feeling been so real.

"Had Matthew *really* needed help? Was his load *really* heavy? Does God *really* answer prayers? Would I ever know for sure?

"Through our only form of communication, a letter, I told Matthew about my walk and God's message to me. Had he needed help? Was he carrying a heavy load? Was the time of my walk the time of his need?

"Two weeks later, I had my answers.

"Matthew wrote, 'God's time is funny because on Wednesday, you helped me carry my rucksack on my eight mile march mostly uphill through the sand. I prayed 'God give me strength and heart to push on', and soon I didn't recognize the weight on my back. I reached around to be sure I hadn't dropped it! God is so awesome".

"God <u>*really does*</u> answer prayers!"

THANK YOU, LORD!!

Ruth was wrestling with God, just like Jacob did. (See Genesis 32: 22-32) I also have experienced times when I wrestled with God and He won out with me, too!

Every day life events; are they worth a THANK YOU, LORD? I think they are. However, I seriously question how many of us take a moment to thank the Lord. The Lord has been faithful in blessing us in many ways and through this process, we grow closer to Jesus Christ. With a close relationship, it's easier to talk to Him and to thank Him for our joys and hardships. However, as we get closer in our relationship with one and another, we often forget to say, "Thank You" as we should. The following story dramatically points out we should say:

"THANK YOU, LORD"

A Story Of St. Peter

St. Peter met a newly arrived soul in Heaven. He toured the soul around Heaven. Both of them walked side-by-side inside a large workroom filled with angels.

St. Peter stopped in front of the first section and said, "This is the Receiving Section. Here, all the petitions to God said in prayer are received." The soul looked at the section. It was terribly busy with so many angels sorting out petitions written on voluminous sheets of paper from all the people of the world.

They walked again until they reached the second section. St. Peter told the soul, "This is the Packaging and Delivery Section. Here, the graces and blessings that the people asked for are packed and delivered to those who asked for them down on earth." The soul saw how busy it was. Many angels worked in that room, since so many blessings were being packed and delivered to Earth.

Finally, at the farthest corner of the room, the soul stopped at the last section. To the surprise of the soul, only one angel stood there idly, doing nothing. "This is the Acknowledging Section," St. Peter told the soul.

"How is it that there is no work here?"

"That's the sad thing," St. Peter answered. "After the people receive the blessings that they asked for, very few send their acknowledgments."

"How does one acknowledge God's blessings?"

"Simple," St. Peter answered. "Just say, 'Thank you, Lord'."

(Reprinted from Touching The Nations website, January 3, 2007; www.touchingthenations.com Author unknown; used by permission.)

CHAPTER 11 –
Memories Good or Bad?

What are memories? The New College Edition of The American Heritage Dictionary defines memories as:

1) The mental faculty of retaining and recalling past experiences; the ability to remember
2) An act or instance of remembrance; a recollection
3) All that a person can remember
4) Something remembered of a person, thing, or event

In other words, memories are simply a recall of experiences - good or bad!

David Seamands has written a book, *Healing of Memories*. He has some interesting experiences with memories. On page 17, he relates that memories can begin before birth.

Everyone's situation and experiences are unique. Each person should be considered as a unique individual made in God's image. However, the experiences related in this book can be used to enlighten one on the effect of memories, good or bad. Memories affect many aspects of life. Good memories give us comfort when recalled. But, bad memories can cause us pain and confusion. The best way to alleviate this pain and confusion is through daily meditation in the word of God.

I believe this can best be accomplished through the Holy Spirit. When our painful memories are released and the Holy Spirit enters our life, change begins.

Generational Curse- What Is It?

Many years ago at one of our Saturday evening concerts at the Des Plaines Methodist Campground, I learned that a performer's wife was sick and not able to attend with him. In further discussion with him, I believed her sickness could have been caused by a "generational curse". This was mentioned to the performer. He was not familiar with the subject. Many people are not acquainted with generational curses.

> *"For I, the Lord your God, am a jealous God, punishing the children for the sin of the fathers to the third and fourth generation of those who hate me, but showing love to a thousand generations, of those who love me and keep my commandments."* *(Exodus 20:4 -6 NIV)*

This is another of the mysteries of God. Why does He punish the children for the father's sins? I thought God was a loving God and we should have a personal relationship with Him. WHY for the father's sins to the third and fourth generation? This whole question of why reminds me of the saying from earlier in this book. "If I understood all the whys of life, I would be God, and since I am not God I do not have to be concerned about all the whys." (Author Unknown) However, that does not stop me from asking, "Why?".

The study notes in the NIV Bible explained verse five in part as:

"Those Israelites who blatantly violate God's covenant and thus show that they reject the Lord as their King will bring down judgment on themselves and their households -- households were usually extended to 'three or four' generations."

A generational curse is one that can extend for several generations.

It can be an alcohol, drug, abuse, anger, negative attitude or any other addiction. Actually the Bible does not talk about addictions. Is it possible that "stronghold" is a better word than "addiction"?

Such a curse can and must, be broken by prayer. After breaking this chain, through prayer and by loving the Lord, a generational blessing to a thousand generations can be received.

> *"...showing love to a thousand generations of those who love me and keep my commandments." (Exodus 20:6 NIV)*

Many questions come to my mind when I think of memories. Are there more good or bad memories? Are bad memories easier to forget? Do we remember everything? Can we ever truly forget? Is God enough?

How can the Holy Spirit help?

Many of the following thoughts are gathered from my friend Eric Schlatterer, and inspirations from the Holy Spirit. Many of my thoughts have been "heavenly inspirations" as I do not know where they came from, other than a word from the Holy Spirit.

Memories

DO THERE TEND TO BE MORE 'GOOD ONES' or 'BAD ONES'?

Eric related that his memories tended "to be more good than bad since I started my walk with the Lord (in earnest) at the beginning of 2003. With time, the good memories have increased while the bad ones have decreased."

I believe, the walk with the Lord has been a major factor in his tendency to have more good than bad memories.

When we walk with the Lord, our memories benefit. We tend to bury many bad memories and it is these bad memories that cause a person to feel like a prisoner in "their own individual prison". When Paul was imprisoned, he had nothing but memories. They helped him break free. The Holy Spirit can help us to break out of "our own individual prison". By resting in the Spirit and walking with the Lord, our "prison" doors of bad memories can be opened.

ARE BAD MEMORIES EASIER TO REPRESS AND BECOME INFECTED THAN GOOD ONES?

We want to forget the bad memories more than we do the good ones. However, the bad memories are more difficult to repress as they keep rising to the surface, like oil on water. Quite often, we rehearse, over and over, our bad memories. Therefore, we get infected with negative attitudes. When negative attitudes get into our thought process our outlook on life becomes very cloudy and before long people don't like to be around us. Just like when we get a physical infection we are put in isolation, so as not to infect someone else. This is what our friends do to us unconsciously.

Having been through six operations in the past six years, I wholeheartedly agree, if no infection develops, it is a successful operation. However, two of my operations resulted in an infection. Unless the infection is cleared up, as it was in my case, the person can die. This is what actually happened to two of my friends; their infections caused their deaths. Just as a physical infection can cause the body's death, an infected memory can cause death to a fruitful life. If not death- depression, anger, resentment and hatred may develop. Therefore, the release of that memory to the Lord and the healing of that memory by being filled with the Holy Spirit is one of the best solutions.

DO OUR MEMORIES CAUSE US TO REMEMBER EVERYTHING?

Looking at my example of the electrical field, I think God has built into each human a mental or emotional fuse that blows when an accidents happen. A fuse will blow when the circuit is overloaded. I am thankful that my mental fuse was blown when I fell and broke my wrist. I do not remember the actual time of falling. God's mercy spared me that painful memory. However, Eric was not spared. He related that, "I have vivid recollections of the times I have injured myself physically or experienced emotional/spiritual distress."

Eric's comments, differing from mine, highlight the idea that I stated in the beginning of this book; do not believe everything just because it is written in a book. Your experiences, your memories, are valuable. Reflect on others' thoughts and experiences and perhaps even learn from them, but ultimately value your memories. They are yours and they are precious. However, if those memories are causing pain and suffering, release them and find the Comforter.

Can We Ever Truly Forget?

Memories, both good and bad, are always there, waiting to explode into our consciousness. How we deal with them is up to us. Will we let God guide us? Will we choose the comfort of the Holy Spirit?

Eric continued to share his thoughts with me. "Yes!!! I believe that these (bad) memories cannot be forgotten, but the wounds they caused and why they cause them are healed by the Holy Spirit. If something triggers these memories, they will not come with all the emotions originally felt during the experience, since the Holy Spirit has healed the wound. I believe the repressed memories that are not faced (with the help of the Holy Spirit) do manifest themselves in our personalities; I know that from personal experience! The Holy Spirit used my memory … to reveal the cause of my pain; I had forgotten many of the original details until the Holy Spirit revealed them to me." (See Appendix A, "Welcoming the Holy Spirit Into Your Life Is A Wise & Powerful Thing To Do.")

Is God Enough?

Eric commented. "I think we need an earthly counselor, but one who is Bible based and can lead us to the truths that are in the Bible, rather than the lies the enemy has been feeding us. The Holy Spirit might be enough for the mature Christian, one whose faith is stronger and knows in his/her heart that God is the healer not man."

So is God enough? Yes and No! God is the beginning and the end. God is everything. But, sometimes we also need an earthly comforter, one who can guide us along the path when our memories cloud the way. On an automobile trip we still need guideposts and direction signs on the road, even if we have a map.

The Holy Spirit and Memories

HOW CAN THE HOLY SPIRIT HELP US WITH OUR MEMORIES?

Many memories, particularly the bad ones, are so hurtful that we try to repress them and bury them. Sometimes we pushed them so far back in our memory that it looks like we have forgotten them. But then, at the most inopportune time it pops back in our mind and we rehearse it over and over. If we allow the painful memories to fester, they will spread. Many times, an experience may be so devastating that we will bury it so deep we'll not remember it. It is still there subconsciously, ready to pop back into our minds without a moments notice. If we allow ourselves to rehearse our problems over and over in our minds they will become infected and the infection will spread. However, the Holy Spirit is there, ready, willing and able to reveal the secrets of our past and what we have to do to be free of them. If we desire to be made whole, the word of God will gladly set us free, through the Holy Spirit.

CHAPTER 12 –
Being Filled With the Holy Spirit

Jesus said, "I am the way and the truth and the life. No one comes to the Father except through me." (John 14:6 - NIV)

This undoubtedly is the most important chapter of this whole book. People say that God works in many different ways and there are many different ways to God. If you have found the peace that passes all understanding, the peace of Christ in your heart, with your present beliefs; Praise God! Stick with what you are doing! However, if you have questions or are disturbed by life, read this chapter over and over and over again until you understand and are filled with the Holy Spirit.

Allow someone to pray with you to receive the infilling of the Holy Spirit. Be sure that the person you ask to pray with you is ordained by God. Such a person could be clergy or laity, male or female, young or old, or of a different denomination. It is possible that you will not feel any different after being prayed for. Feelings and physical manifestations are not important. What is important is what happens in your belief chamber- your heart. BUT... I believe that you will know, that you know, that you know, without any doubt, when you have experienced the baptism of the Holy Spirit as manifested by resting in the Spirit. Experience counts! A vast majority of people having this experience know for sure that they have been in the presence of Christ. Hence they could not stand in His presence.

Many people who have not had this experience ask, "How will I know if I truly have received the baptism of the Holy Spirit?"

Read on!
You will know, for sure, when it happens.

The first and greatest miracle in life is *salvation*. Many churches teach that you receive the Holy Spirit when you are saved. Regardless of whether this is true or not, it is very important to be saved before being filled with the Holy Spirit. Although it could and has happened that baptism of the Holy Spirit has occurred before salvation, it is not the norm. It is up to God. He is, and always will be, in control.

The Holy Spirit is a gift from the Father. I believe it is best to *know* the Father, through salvation and faith. Get to KNOW God and develop a personal relationship with Him through His Word. Read the Bible and let the Author, the Holy Spirit, be with you for interpretation and enlightenment.

Isn't it more comforting to receive a gift from someone you know? If a stranger were to give you a gift wouldn't you wonder if it was OK to receive it? Or what their motivation was in giving it to you? Since the Holy Spirit is a gift from the Father, I believe it is best to know the Father through salvation and faith rather than just knowing about Him. Get to KNOW God and develop a personal relationship with Him, as a first step to receiving His gift.

The Blessed Assurance Of Salvation

Many people do not have the assurance of their salvation. I look to Romans 10:9-10 for that blessed assurance. I call these verses the 'dynamite verses of the Bible'. Why? These verses can charge you up and set you on fire! Look at the first letter of the words "ten - nine - ten". You get T-N-T; TNT is dynamite. Dynamite carries a huge charge just as these words. I have shared this with many people who I have had the pleasure to associate with through Project Understanding Bail Project and it is one of the most remembered points. TNT – the dynamite verses of the Bible.

> *"That if you confess with your mouth, 'Jesus is Lord,' and believe in your heart that God raised Him from the dead, you will be saved. For it is with your heart*

> *that you believe and are justified, and it is with your*
> *mouth that you confess and are saved."*
> *(Romans 10:9-10 NIV)*

This Is The Blessed Assurance Of Our Salvation

Therefore, if you can say "Jesus is Lord" and believe in your heart that the Heavenly Father raised His Son, Jesus, from the tomb, you are saved.

If you have any question about your salvation, say to yourself, right now wherever you may be, "Jesus Is Lord". Believe it! Truly believe that Jesus is your Lord and Savior. Also believe that God raised Jesus from the dead. Then you are saved! You have the assurance of the Word of God of your salvation.

"For it is with your heart that you believe ..." (Romans 10:10 NIV) Therefore, that makes your heart your belief chamber, NOT your head. The longest distance in the world is the 18 inches from your head to your heart! Your head is your REASONING chamber and your heart is your BELIEF chamber. You cannot reason Christianity; you can only reason religion. You must BELIEVE that Jesus is Lord. You must have faith! Remember the difference between Christianity and religion?

CHRISTIANITY is a personal relationship with Jesus Christ and RELIGION is a belief in a doctrine.

After you have the assurance of salvation, read Acts 1:4-5.

> *"On one occasion, while He (Jesus) was eating with them (the disciples), He gave them this command: 'Do not leave Jerusalem, but wait for the gift my Father promised, which you have heard me speak about. For John baptized with water, but in a few days you will be baptized with the Holy Spirit'. (Acts 1: 4- 5 NIV)*

These two verses have five important points.

1- DO NOT LEAVE JERUSALEM, stay there,

2- WAIT for the gift,

3- The GIFT is for you, THE FATHER HAS PROMISED IT,

4- John's baptism was the WATER BAPTISM and

5- You will be baptized with the HOLY SPIRIT.

Let's look at these five points in greater detail.

Do Not Leave Jerusalem; Stay In Jerusalem

Why did Jesus tell his disciples to stay in Jerusalem? I did not know and the majority of people I ask do not know. E. Stanley Jones has written a great explanation for this question.

> *"...the disciples' greatest problem was Jerusalem. Jerusalem was the center of both political and*

> *religious hostility – so hostile that they (the political and religious community) combined and crucified their Lord. Before the storm of that awful hostility, the disciples bent and some broke in betrayal and denial. …Jerusalem was the place of their failure; there they all forsook Him and fled…here was Jesus asking them to walk up to their most difficult problem – Jerusalem - face it and master it. …And having mastered Jerusalem, they were ready for anything."* (E. Stanley Jones, 1884-1973; © 1955; ISBN 0-687-23734-3; © renewal 1983; pages 23- 24)

Shortly after reading this, the Lord showed me that most everyone in the world has his or her own 'Jerusalem'. Everyone includes you and me; we all have our own Jerusalem. Therefore, it is important to master our Jerusalem before we can be filled with the Holy Spirit as manifested by resting in the Spirit. The best way to master our Jerusalem is to turn it (our secret burden) over to the Lord. Release it! Cast your cares upon HIM.

> *"Cast all your anxiety on Him, because He cares for you." (1 Peter 5:7 NIV)*

Release your burden to Him!
Release your Jerusalem to JESUS!

What Is My Jerusalem?

You may ask, what exactly is my Jerusalem? It is a hang-up or a burden. It could be simple or very, very complex. It could be an addiction to food, alcohol, drugs, sex, work, television or any idol that you may have. It could be having experienced sexual abuse, physical abuse and/or mental abuse sometime in your life. It could be guilt, unforgiveness, hatred, anger, or resentment for something that someone might have said to you or did to you at one time. It could be a parent that told you that you were too fat, or not as smart as your brother or sister, or that you would never amount to anything. It could be as simple as a teacher saying in front of the whole class, "I explained that during the lesson; now go back to your seat and do it."

Your Jerusalem could even be pre-natal, a before-birth event or an early childhood memory, deeply buried in your mind. It could be fresh, something that happened recently and is right on the top of your mind. Your Jerusalem could be anything that is causing you pain or is a burden to you. Possibly, you don't even know you have a Jerusalem.

This was the case for one man who came forward for prayer ministry. When asked for his prayer request, he said he wanted the baptism of the Holy Spirit. After explaining Acts 1:4-5, I asked if he had a burden, a

Jerusalem, which should be released to the Lord. He did not know of anything. So we prayed for him to receive the infilling of the Holy Spirit. After being filled with the Holy Spirit, as manifested by resting in the Spirit, he got up exclaiming, "I got the answer".

"What was the question?" I replied.

He explained that quite a while ago, he had purchased a new vehicle and his brother had borrowed it. While driving it, his brother was involved in a fatal accident. He never knew if his brother had accepted the Lord as his Savior and he was wondering where the brother was, in heaven or hell. While resting in the Spirit he saw his brother's face and KNEW that he was in heaven. He had received the answer to his long forgotten question; where is my brother? He had released a Jerusalem that he hadn't even realized he carried!

You may be in the same situation. You may be carrying your Jerusalem, a burden, and not be aware of it. On the other hand, you may know all too well about your Jerusalem. Whichever the case, go to prayer and ask the Lord to show you your Jerusalem. Ask Him to help you release your burden and to feel His peace. Jesus says,

> *"Peace I leave with you; my peace I give you. I do not give to you as the world gives. Do not let your hearts be troubled and do not be afraid."*
> *(John 14:27 NIV)*

When releasing your Jerusalem, symbolically raise your hands. Offer your burden to God and He will take it. Some people have excitedly shared their comments on this experience:

"When I raised my hands, I felt my burden going out through my fingertips on their way to God" and "When I reached up as far as I could, I felt God's hand coming down the rest of the way and touching the palm of my hands with His fingers."

So, REACH UP as high as you can. GOD will REACH DOWN the rest of the way and TOUCH YOU! Many times when people release their burdens, by symbolically reaching up to God, they rest in the Spirit before having a prayer for the infilling of the Holy Spirit.

When Jesus said, "Do not leave Jerusalem", He was asking his disciples to walk up to their most difficult problem, their Jerusalem, to face it and master it. Of course, Jesus knew they couldn't do it on their own, so he sent the Holy Spirit with His awesome, promised power.

> *"But you will receive power when the Holy Spirit comes upon you, ..." (Acts 1: 8a NIV)*

He was going to make the place of their greatest failure the place of their greatest success. Had the disciples not accepted the responsibility of facing their Jerusalem, they would have been running around in circles instead of joyously undertaking the assigned task. Just like the disciples, you can face your Jerusalem (your most difficult problem, memory or burden) and master it in Jesus name. When you do that, you will be ready to face anything and master it in His name.

Face your Jerusalem!

See Appendix E- Pastor Tim Roames message entitled "The Prayer of Release" is an excellent preparation to receiving the Holy Spirit.

Wait For The Gift

With this promise, as with many in the Bible, we must do something first to receive the promise. In this case, we must <u>wait</u>. Sometimes we do not know what we are waiting for or how long we must wait.

The best way to wait is to get into the Word of God, the Bible, and develop a closer relationship with God. No matter how close a relationship you presently have with God, you can always have a closer relationship with Him. Through that closer relationship, God will begin to communicate with you. He may communicate through prayer, a still small voice, or through another person.

Wait expectantly!

> *"The people were waiting expectantly and were all wondering in their hearts if John might possibly be the Christ." (Luke 3: 15 NIV)*

Who Needs A Comforter, Volume 2 will have a chapter on the subject of EQ (Expectancy Quotient). We hear a lot about IQ, Intelligence Quotient, but little about EQ. Look forward to more about EQ.

WAIT EXPECTANTLY!!

The Gift Has Been Promised By The Father

The PROMISE OF THE FATHER was and <u>is</u> the gift of the Holy Spirit that is given to every believer. That promise is for eternal life when we die and the divine energy and power of God to experience the abundant life here on earth. Jesus received the fullness of God as He was exalted. He gives that to us by sending the promised Holy Spirit. It is through the power of the Holy Spirit that Jesus' fullness flows to us and through us to the world, to the glory and honor of God.

When we are promised something, we have to trust and believe that the person will live up to their promise. The Father and Son have never made a promise that they did not keep. When we receive a gift we must reach out and accept it, with open hands. It is the same with the Holy Spirit; we must accept Him with open hands, open mind and open heart. We must put Him into our heart. Remember your heart is the belief chamber. It is here that the Holy Spirit resides.

> *"I am leaving you with a gift -- peace of mind and heart!" (John 14:27- The Living Bible)*

Water Baptism–John's Baptism

> *" ... John came, baptizing in the desert region and preaching a baptism of repentance for the forgiveness of sins." (Mark 1:4 NIV)*

> *"And this was his message: 'After me will come one more powerful than I, the thongs of whose sandals I am not worthy to stoop down and untie. I baptize you with water but He will baptize you with the Holy Spirit' " (Mark 1:7-8 NIV)*

Water baptism is a baptism of repentance. Through this act, we are washed clean of our sins and forgiven for our actions. Water immersion, or total immersion, appears to me to be the most meaningful expression of water baptism. Symbolically, in water baptism by immersion, one dies to self, our crucifixion, when going down into the water and upon rising from the water, a new person arises. Just like Jesus Christ's resurrection after his crucifixion, we are resurrected a new person with ALL of our sins forgiven. God will forget our sins. He does not keep a record of them. We need to do the same!

We need to cast all our sins and burdens (our Jerusalems) symbolically, into the deepest ocean and post a NO FISHING sign. Many people release their sins and burdens to Jesus, but they keep fishing them back into their life. They keep trying to be in control. Remember Jesus Christ is in control, not we ourselves. He will not remember your sins and burdens once you release them to Him. Cast out your sins and stop fishing for them. You do not have to rehearse them over and over. Leave them with Him!

You Will Be Baptized With The Holy Spirit

In Jesus' day, John the Baptist performed water baptism. Today clergy perform it. Both John the Baptist and clergy are considered preparers of the way for the Lord.

> *"As it is written in the words of Isaiah the prophet:*
> *'A voice of one calling in the desert,' "Prepare the*
> *way for the Lord, make straight paths for Him".*
> *(Luke 3: 4 NIV)*

John 3 is one of the most powerful chapters in the Bible and possibly one of the most confusing. I believe that John 3:3-8, is very clear when the eyes of your heart are opened by the Holy Spirit.

> *"In reply Jesus declared, 'I tell you the truth, no one can see the kingdom of God unless he is born again.' 'How can a man be born when he is old?', Nicodemus asked. 'Surely he cannot enter a second time into his mother's womb to be born!' Jesus answered, 'I tell you the truth; no one can enter the kingdom of God unless he is born of water and the Spirit. Flesh gives birth to flesh, but the Spirit gives birth to spirit. You should not be surprised at my saying, 'You must be born again.' The wind blows wherever it pleases. You hear its sound, but you cannot tell where it comes from or where it is going. So it is with everyone born of the Spirit.' " (John 3:3-8 NIV)*

Jesus Christ is the baptizer of the Holy Spirit.

> *"He (Jesus Christ) will baptize you with the Holy Spirit and with fire" (Luke 3:16b NIV).*

When you come into the presence of Jesus Christ to receive His baptism of the Holy Spirit, I believe it is very difficult to stand. Therefore, I believe *resting* in the Spirit is a very important part of the baptism of the Holy Spirit. Until one personally experiences the Baptism of the Holy Spirit as manifested by resting in the Spirit, understanding and believing is difficult. Remember, the head knows but the heart believes! However, I believe it is not necessary to rest in the Spirit to be filled with the Holy Spirit. But, if you wish to have the fullness of what God has for you, you must completely surrender everything to God, die to self and get out of control. Let God be in control; and expect God to come in all His fullness into your life.

Also, anyone who is going to pray for someone else to receive the baptism of the Holy Spirit as manifested by resting in the Spirit, should have personally had this experience. I fail to see how one person can pass on to another person something they have not received.

I remember the United Methodist Bishop of Cuba speaking at an Aldersgate Holy Spirit Conference. He said he would not send a pastor out into the field until he, the Bishop, had the assurance that the pastor had experienced the baptism of the Holy Spirit. I wholeheartedly agree. However, I would add that they should experience resting in the Spirit.

Now, the question from the beginning of the chapter; How will I know if I have truly received the baptism of the Holy Spirit?

The short answer, experience it! Only by having the experience of resting in the Spirit can you truly know.

The long answer:

1. Re-read this chapter, particularly the section, "You Will Be Baptized With The Holy Spirit."

2. Get into the Word and let the Word get into you.

3. Get into a small group at your local church. If your church does not have a small group, start one.

4. Increase your EQ (Expectancy Quotient)

5. Look forward to more experiences of healing, forgiveness, and deliverance. Look forward to Who Needs A Comforter? Volume 2 and 3.

CHAPTER 13 –
Why Should I "Rest In The Spirit"?

I have mentioned many times throughout this book, about people receiving the Baptism of the Holy Spirit, as manifested by resting in the Spirit. I hope that this has caused you to ask some questions. Have you wondered? Is Baptism of the Holy Spirit necessary for eternal life? Is Baptism of the Holy Spirit necessary for a personal relationship with Jesus Christ? Will I be a better person if I receive the Baptism of the Holy Spirit? Why should I rest in the Spirit? Who is the baptizer? What benefits and/or blessings are available to me if I receive the Baptism of the Holy Spirit, as manifested by resting in the Spirit? We will look more closely at each of these questions after we look more closely at the Holy Spirit.

In the beginning of this book, I asked you not to accept everything that people say, including me, without considering your opinions, your beliefs, your experiences, your conscience and God's word, the Bible. Please remember this as we examine the phenomenon of resting in the Spirit.

Many religions speak of the God of Abraham, Isaac and Jacob or a god but do not mention Jesus Christ or the Holy Spirit. Just as you can't do everything in your life by yourself, God didn't want to do everything by Himself. Therefore, Jesus Christ, God's only son, came into being and God allowed him to come to earth as man, to be a role model for all mankind. When Jesus Christ had to leave earth and go to be with the Father, He knew WE couldn't do "it" by ourselves. What is "it"? "It" is the abundant life that was promised to us, if we believe. Since we needed help Jesus gave us the Holy Spirit:

> *"And I will ask the Father, and He will give you another Counselor to be with you forever- the Spirit of truth. The world cannot accept Him, because it neither sees Him or knows Him. But you know Him, for He lives with you and will be in you. (John 14: 16-17 NIV).*

The Holy Spirit knew we couldn't do "it" on our own so He gave us the Spiritual gifts of wisdom, knowledge, faith, healing, miraculous powers, prophecy, distinguishing between spirits, speaking in tongues and interpretation of tongues. If we accept the Holy Spirit into our lives, these gifts are ours. Just like Jesus Christ, we must someday leave this earth; so we need someone to carry on. Just as Jesus Christ performed no miracles or Ministry until he received power from on high; neither can you nor I.

When we get out of the way, by releasing our greatest burden or burdens - the ones we have kept secret for many,

many years - then the baptizer Jesus Christ, can come into our lives and fill us with the Holy Spirit. Be FILLED with the Spirit!

Usually He does not fill us without performing spiritual surgery to remove those long-held thoughts or burdens that we have harbored in our hearts. If you have ever had physical surgery, you know there are precautions and preparations before moving into the operating room. We do not just walk in, jump on the table, and say, "Ok, Doc. Let's get started!" No, we need preparation and assistance from knowledgeable doctors and nurses. God wants us to have successful physical surgery for better health and likewise he wants us to have successful spiritual surgery. However, many times we "stand" in the way instead of allowing His presence to come into our lives. Our past hurts and burdens are a mountainous barrier that must be removed or released to the Lord.

> *"…I tell you the truth, if you have faith as small as a mustard seed, you can say to this mountain, 'Move from here to there' and it will move. Nothing will be impossible for you." (Matthew 17: 20b-21 NIV)*

During physical surgery, the anesthesiologist usually monitors the drugs that put us to sleep. During spiritual surgery, God knows we will listen more intently to His voice if we are resting in the arms of Christ or "resting in the Spirit".

Many have asked why do people fall to the floor when they receive the baptism of the Holy Spirit? One pastor I know says, "Because they can't stand." Well, of course but on a more serious note, I believe that when Jesus Christ truly comes into your life, by your *complete* surrender of self, and His presence is experienced, you cannot stand. Now that I have said that, I must add that it is not necessary to fall to the floor when one experiences the baptism of the Holy Spirit. One time a youth pastor, who received the baptism of the Holy Spirit in our Chapel, could not move for 10 minutes. When I asked him what happened he said that he tried to lift his feet but couldn't. It was as if his feet were 'nailed' to the floor. There are **many** ways for God to get our attention.

Now, let's get back to the questions raised earlier. Is Baptism of the Holy Spirit necessary for eternal life? No, everyone will have eternal life so the Baptism of the Holy Spirit is not a prerequisite for eternal life. Some will go to hell and be with Satan. Some will go to heaven and be with Jesus Christ.

Which place are you planning to be?
Smoking or Non-Smoking?

Is Baptism of the Holy Spirit necessary for a personal relationship with Jesus Christ? No, but the Baptism of the Holy Spirit will give us a closer relationship with

Jesus Christ. It is not mandatory but it gives us MORE benefits. Life will be better and more complete with the Holy Spirit in it!

Will I be a better person if I receive the Baptism of the Holy Spirit? Yes, you will get to know the author of the Word. You will better understand God's word, the Bible. You will be better able to handle the ups and downs of life. Assuming you have released your long-held burden or burdens, God will be able to bless you with MORE abundance.

Why should I rest in the Spirit? So God can have your undivided attention and you can hear His still small voice. He will prepare you for unity with Him and others. He will prepare you for MORE.

> *"I have given them the glory that You gave Me, that they may be one as We are one; I in them and You in Me. May they be brought to complete unity to let the world know that you sent me and have loved them even as You have loved Me. Father, I want those you have given Me to be with Me where I am, and to see my glory, the glory you have given me because you loved me before the creation of the world."* (John 17:22- 24 NIV)

John 17 is Jesus' prayer for Himself, His disciples and all believers, that includes you and me, if we believe in Jesus Christ.

Who is the baptizer? Jesus Christ is the baptizer, who is manifested through the person praying with you. In this instance, the person praying with you is an instrument of God. It is not mandatory to have someone pray with you to receive the Holy Spirit. You can be alone and pray to receive the Baptism of the Holy Spirit, in your private, personal place of prayer.

What benefits and/or blessings are available to me if I receive the Baptism of the Holy Spirit, as manifested by resting in the Spirit? When you are resting in the arms of Christ, He will give you peace. You will experience a peace like one you have never felt before. As people get back on their feet, I ask them what they felt when they rested in the arms of Christ? Most often, their response is "peace".

> *"Peace I leave with you; my peace I give you."* *(John 14:27a NIV)*

The biggest and greatest benefit of the Baptism of the Holy Spirit, as manifested by resting in the spirit, is the FRUIT, which develops as you utilize your new gift from the Father.

> *"But the fruit of the Spirit is love, joy, peace, patience, kindness, goodness, faithfulness, gentleness and self-control."* *(Galatians 5:22 – 23a NIV)*

The fruit of the Spirit is LOVE. All other characteristics, joy, peace, patience, kindness, goodness, faithfulness, gentleness and self-control are amplified by the LOVE of God that you receive through the Baptism of the Holy Spirit. The more you utilize your new gift at home, work, school, and church, the more you will be blessed. You will be blessed MORE & MORE when you show this new gift of LOVE to your friends and family!

There is no limit to what God can do and will do for us.

CHAPTER 14 –
A Challenge

Why Do Some People, Like Me,
Ask A Lot Of Questions?

Some people are naturally more inquisitive than others and ask many questions. My wife feels that I ask too many questions, some that are not necessary and some that are just annoying. That may be, but asking questions is how I learn. Asking many questions also helps me think in a different way than many people and outside the normal boundaries that society and worldly education puts around us. This comment brought to memory a puzzle that has stumped many people. Give it a try and you will see why!

The object is to connect all nine o's by four straight lines without taking your pen or pencil off the paper.

It can be done!

The solution to the puzzle is at the back of this book.

O   O   O

O   O   O

O   O   O

Clue to the solution - remember to think in a different way and to think outside the normal boundaries that society and worldly education puts around us.

If everyone did not have an inquisitive and searching mind how would we have new discoveries, new products, a better way of life and new ideas? Of course, not all people need to be the inquisitive type, but those who are, need to have the freedom to ask questions and delve into the region of the unknown. The information explosion of the current day would make one question whether there would be anything new to discover or uncover. However, I believe there are many areas of life that have not even been scratched. Possibly, we don't need to understand ALL of the causes or ALL of the Whys in life. (See chapter 3) One such area, is often called "acts of God" such as miracles, some healings, floods and earthquakes, such as the one that created the December 2004 tsunami in the Indian Ocean. One recent article that I read claimed that this tsunami experience caused an adjustment to the earth's crust. It was claimed that this adjustment moved the island of Sumatra 100 feet to the southwest and sped up the earth's rotation by three microseconds. Such power is beyond the human mind's comprehension, yet scientists should continue to explore and uncover, by questioning, these devastating events. How are new things discovered or uncovered if everyone accepts the current day knowledge as being sufficient?

Most churches and mainline denominations have stated that all believers receive the Holy Spirit when they are saved. This may be the case, BUT I have a question.

Is There More Of God Available To Us?

If there is and I believe there is, our churches need to talk more about the Holy Spirit. I propose that the Holy Spirit, in ALL of His fullness, is the missing link to receiving more of God.

I would like to leave you with several thoughts as a final challenge.

IS IT POSSIBLE THAT YOU MAY NOT RECEIVE THE COMPLETE FULLNESS OF THE FATHER'S PROMISE OF THE HOLY SPIRIT WHEN YOU ARE SAVED (CONVERTED, REDEEMED, BECOME A FOLLOWER OF CHRIST OR WHATEVER TERM YOU MAY USE)?

DO WE NEED SUPERNATURAL HELP (POWER AND ENERGY) TO LIVE ABUNDATELY AS A MORE COMPLETED CHRISTIAN?

COULD THE BAPTISM OF THE HOLY SPIRIT, AS MANIFESTED BY RESTING IN THE SPIRIT, BE A SECONDARY BLESSING FROM GOD?

(OTHER MANIFESTATIONS WILL BE DISCUSSED IN VOLUME 2 OF *WHO NEEDS A COMFORTER?*)

IS IT POSSIBLE THAT A MORE COMPLETED CHRISTIAN NEEDS TO BE AND WILL BE REFILLED WITH THE HOLY SPIRIT EVERY DAY OF HIS OR HER LIFE?

I believe the answer to all four areas of this challenge is the same, "**YES**"!

As my good Catholic friend from Full Gospel Business Men's Fellowship told me. "I will not defend or debate the scriptures with you; I will let the Holy Spirit do that for you, the same as He has done for me."

In order for the Holy Spirit to convict you of anything, He must come into your heart, into your belief chamber. If you are not sure that the Holy Spirit is part of your life, part of your heart, re-read Chapter 12; follow the directions in the chapter or contact the author.

WHO NEEDS A COMFORTER?

EVERYONE !

APPENDIX A –
Welcoming the Holy Spirit
Into Your Life

Is A Wise & Powerful Thing To Do

Message given by Pastor Tim Roames on December 5, 2004. This is one of the finest talks on the subject of the Holy Spirit that I have heard in my lifetime. The following is just a brief outline of Pastor Tim's presentation.

TITLE: "Welcoming The Holy Spirit Into Your Life Is A Wise & Powerful Thing To Do"

1) When God's Spirit moved upon the earth great things were about to happen.Genesis 1:1 – 3
2) God's Word and the Holy Spirit working together did great things. John 1:14

Some believe the Holy Spirit "Camp" is more important than the Word "Camp". One without the other is not as powerful as the combination.

3) Jesus was the Living Word. He performed no miracles until He was baptized in the River Jordan by John and was filled with the Spirit.
4) When the Holy Spirit came upon Jesus great things happened.

5) The disciples had the Word of God, yet they waited on the Holy Spirit. Luke 24:46 – 49

6) When the Holy Spirit came upon the disciples, great things happened and they received power. Acts 2:1-4

7) We need the Word of God in our lives. You also need the Holy Spirit in your life. (See author's note at the end of this summary.)

8) We need the Holy Spirit and the Word together. Luke 24:49

9) You can invite the Holy Spirit into your life. No other spirit will get on you. (Some religions profess that if you ask God for the Holy Spirit that you might get any kind of spirit, including evil ones.)

The turning point for Pastor Tim was when he saw Luke 11:13.

> *"If you then, though you are evil, know how to give good gifts to your children, how much more will your Father in heaven give the Holy Spirit to those who ask Him!" (Luke 11: 13 NIV)*

10) There are reasons why the Holy Spirit does not move in your life.

A) You are unaware it is available.

B) You are not open to it or don't want it.

C) You reject the Word. Mark 3:1-7

11) Three steps to being open and sensitive to the Holy Spirit.

A) Decide to live for God. Decide that you need the Holy Spirit.

    I) Live by The Command of Love (Living the Word) Forgive and Walk in Love.

    II) Learn and decide to live by Faith in God's Word.

B) Get rid of sin - Confess it. Confusion is not of God.

C) Pray and ask God for his Holy Spirit.

12) Mary said, "Be it unto me according to thy Word". *May we ask for the power and the Holy Spirit according to the Word. (Luke 24:49)*

To purchase a copy of Pastor Tim Roames' message go to www.GoodNewsChristianCenter.org

Or order by snail mail at:

Good News Christian Center

815 Lee St

Des Plaines, IL 60016

Phone: (847) 390 – 5840

Cost is $4.00 plus shipping

Comments By Author–

Pastor Tim said, "We need the Word of God in our lives. You also need the Holy Spirit in your life" (#7 above).

I also believe that we do receive the Holy Spirit when we are saved. But, the Word also says

> *"… how much more will your Father in heaven give the Holy Spirit to those who ask him!" (Luke 11:13)*

So, according to the Word of God it is possible to ask God for the baptism of the Holy Spirit and to be filled with the Holy Spirit. For one example of how to be filled with the Holy Spirit, see Chapter 12. Possibly you need to ask an anointed child of God to pray with you to receive the infilling (or the refilling) of the Holy Spirit. I believe, as we become more and more surrendered to God, we can receive more and more blessings through the Holy Spirit.

Jesus began his ministry only after being baptized (Luke 3:21-23). He did no miracles until he was baptized and full of the Holy Spirit (Luke 4:1). Jesus did not do it on His own and neither can you or I.

You Need The Power Of The Holy Spirit

> *"…. you will receive power when the Holy Spirit comes on you; and you will be my witnesses in Jerusalem, and in all Judea and Samaria, and to the ends of the earth". (Acts 1: 8 NIV)*

APPENDIX B –
Holy Spirit

Background Information

HOSEA 4:6   (Lack of Knowledge)

ACTS 19:2   (Disciples did not know)

Baptism of Water- Baptism of Repentance and What You Receive

ACTS 19:3-4   (John's Baptism)

ACTS 22:16   (Wash Clean)

MARK 1:4   (Forgiveness)

LUKE 3:3   (Forgiveness)

Why Baptism of the Spirit?

JOHN 3:3 & 3:5-8   (To See Kingdom of God)

I CORINTHIANS 12:13   (One Body)

MARK 1:7-8   (John Preaches)

Baptism of the Holy Spirit:

ACTS 19:5-6   (Of the Disciples)

ACTS 1:5   (Promise of God)

ACTS 8:14-17   (Samarians Receive)

ACTS 11:16   (Word of the Lord)

GALATIANS 4:6   (Into Our Heart)

LUKE 3:16   (Christ Will Do It)

God's Promise of the Gift:

ACTS 1:4   (Last Command of Jesus)
ACTS 2:38   (Peter Addresses the Crowd)
EPHESIANS 1:13   (Spiritual Blessings in Christ)

The Work of the Holy Spirit:

JOHN 14: 16-17   (Counselor – Spirit of Truth)
JOHN 16: 7-15   (Ministry)

What Benefits Do You Receive From the Holy Spirit?

ACTS 1:8 & 10:38   (Power)
ACTS 2:4 & 10:44-46   (Tongues)
GALATIANS 5:22   (Fruit of the Spirit)
ROMANS 8:1-39   (Freedom-Strength in a New Life)

ROMANS 8:26-27   (Intercessor in Prayer)
I CORINTHIANS 2:6-16   (Wisdom)
JOHN 14:26   (Comfort and Teachings)
I CORINTHIANS 12:1-11   (Spiritual Gifts)
ACTS 4:31   (Speak Boldly)
II TIMOTHY 1:6-7   (Power, Love and Self-discipline)

Can You Buy the Benefits of the Holy Spirit?

ACTS 8:18-22   (Simon's attempt)

Jesus began his ministry after being baptized (see Luke 3:21-23); He did no miracles until he was baptized and full of the Holy Spirit (see Luke 4:1); Jesus didn't do it on His own and neither can you or I.

Compiled by Charles E. Cilley, Sr. - 1997 (Revised 2005)

APPENDIX C –
Spirit Empowered Life

In the Old Testament, the Spirit of God, the manifestation of the one God working in creation and in human beings, is referred to about 80 times. In the New Testament, it is referred to 240 times. The Holy Spirit is the source of strength of mighty men, the inspiration of rulers and prophets. The Holy Spirit often produces unexpected results (I Kings 18:12; II Kings 2:16; Ezekiel 8:3-11). The Holy Spirit also gives the gift of intelligence and artistic endowments (Daniel 5:14).

The Holy Spirit's first interaction with Jesus in the New Testament was in Matthew 3:16. By the power of the Holy Spirit, Jesus worked miracles (Matthew 12:28; Acts 10:38) and taught His disciples (Acts 1:2). John recorded Jesus' promise to his disciples that the Holy Spirit would be sent to them to remind them of Jesus' words and to enable them to bear witness to Him. This came to pass immediately after the resurrection (John 20:22) and then in a fuller way 47 days later on the day of Pentecost (Acts 1:8; Acts 2:1-4). Pentecost has often been considered the birth of the church.

The New Testament teaches that the Holy Spirit is active in the believer of Jesus, to give the believer a new birth, (Titus 3:5; John 3:5-8), to endow the believer with spiritual gifts for the good of the entire body of believers (I Corinthians 12:4-12) and to produce in him those traits of character which will make the believer like Christ. For this purpose, the Spirit of God is said to "dwell in" every person who believes in Jesus. (Romans 8:9-11).

The Holy Spirit is the third person of the Trinity. The formula of Matthew 28:19 clearly ranks the Holy Spirit with the Father and Son as God, in whose name Christian baptism is performed. Each person of the Trinity is fully and equally God. Yet each is distinct, and each has a distinctive role in carrying out the plan of salvation. In performing His role, the Holy Spirit is said to be sent by both the Father (John 14:26) and the Son (John 15:26). In performing His ministry, the Holy Spirit is committed to exalting Jesus Christ rather than Himself (John 16:13-15). Just as Jesus submitted to the will of the Father (Matthew 26:39) so the Holy Spirit submits Himself to the Father and the Son.

The relationship of the Holy Spirit to righteous living is also expressed in Psalm 51:10-11.

Written by a friend, Marty, of the Wheaton, IL., chapter of FGBMFI. Verbally he gave permission to use 1997.

APPENDIX D –
At the Cross

I WAS NOT THERE TO CARRY THE CROSS FOR <u>YOU</u>,
SO YOU CARRIED THE CROSS FOR ME.
I COULD NOT HAVE DONE IT WITHOUT <u>YOU</u>.
TO CALVARY <u>YOU</u> WENT- TO RECONCILE IT ALL.

THE SOLDIERS CRIED, "IF <u>YOU</u> ARE THE SON OF GOD
COME DOWN FROM THE CROSS".
<u>YOU</u> STAYED TO DO YOUR FATHER'S WILL.
HELP ME TO DO YOUR WILL, O LORD.

TO THE CROSS <u>YOU</u> CAME,
SO I CAN NOW COME,
I COME TO THE CROSS ALONE.
AT THE FOOT OF THE CROSS,
I COME AND BOW.

ON THE CROSS <u>YOU</u> GAVE ALL FOR ME,
NOW AT THE CROSS I GIVE ALL OF ME.
NOTHING BUT THE CROSS OF CHRIST

SHOWS US HOW MUCH WE ARE LOVED.

YOU SAID, "GIVE FREELY- GIVE <u>ME</u> YOUR BURDEN".
I RELEASE IT TO YOU NOW, OH, LORD.
INTO THE VOID CAUSED BY THAT RELEASE,
I ASK YOU TO FILL ME WITH YOUR HOLY
SPIRIT.

COME LORD JESUS, COME HOLY SPIRIT,
THERE IS ALWAYS ROOM FOR MORE OF <u>YOU,</u>
SO COME HOLY SPIRIT- FILL THAT VOID AND
COMFORT ME.

HELP ME TO HOLD ONTO THE CROSS,
WHERE <u>YOUR</u> BLOOD WAS SHED FOR ME.
AS I LEAN ON THE CROSS, AT THE FOOT OF
THE CROSS,
MAY YOUR BLOOD DRIP DOWN UPON ME,
CLEANSING AND REVIVING ME AGAIN.

REJOICE, AGAIN I SAY REJOICE,
IN THE POWER OF THE CROSS.

Written by Charles E. Cilley, Sr.
(Summer, 2005 - while sitting "At The Cross" during early morning prayer, Good News Christian Center, Des Plaines, IL.) Revised May 2006.

APPENDIX E –
The Prayer of Release

I felt this message by Pastor Tim Roames of Good News Christian Center, fell right in line with Chapter 12- Being Filled With The Holy Spirit.

This message was given June 5, 2005.

Release your "Jerusalem". Whether it be guilt, resentment or a self-imposed addiction it doesn't matter. After you release it and cast it upon Jesus, you can be filled with the Holy Spirit and have the peace of Christ.

The following is a brief outline of his presentation.

TITLE: "The Prayer of Release" based on Matthew 6:12 (Point #6 in 'The Model Prayer: Road to Inner Peace' Series)

1) This message is about peace and prayer. The Bible says lasting peace needs communication with God. The Bible calls it prayer and the world calls it communication.

2) Two greatest barriers to having lasting peace are
   A) guilt for what <u>we do</u> in our life, and
   B) resentment for what <u>is done to us</u> in our life

3) The best way to get rid of guilt is to go to God and receive forgiveness from God.

4) The best way to get rid of resentment is to forgive others.

5) In this life you will be hurt, either accidentally or on purpose. It doesn't matter how you got hurt, what matters is how you handle the hurt. Don't dwell on the source.

6) Your hurt can give you peace or pain. If you release it and let go of it, it will give you peace. If you hold onto it and rehearse it over and over, the hurt will give you pain.

7) We must release the hurt or let go of the offense so we can be set free and have peace. We must release the other individual so we can have peace for our self.

8) The question is always asked, "How much do we have to forgive?"

   Peter asked the same question. Refer to Matthew 18:21. The Jewish law said three times. But, in Matthew 18:22 Jesus says 70 times 7.

9) Starting in Matthew 18:23, Jesus tells a parable about a king forgiving a servant a large debt (approximately $12 million in today's money). Then the servant goes out and does <u>not</u> forgive a person who owes him a small debt (approximately $17 in today's money).

How could the King forgive such a large debt?

Because the king was God.

10) What grudge do you have in your heart that you have not released? What memory haunts you that you are not willing to let go of? What hurt is there in your heart that you haven't been able to let go?

11) You may ask, "Why should I forgive?" You say you don't want to release it. I want to hold on to the hurt, the anger, the resentment.

12) There are three reasons why you should let go, release it and forgive.

A) God forgave you,

B) Resentment will make you miserable, and

C) You are going to need forgiveness again.

Biblical references include Matthew 18:27; Matthew 18:33; Joel 5:2; Matthew 5:7 and Joel 11:13-16. A few of the points are

- One person said when you have resentment or unforgiveness against someone, it is like drinking poison and expecting the other person to die.

- Resentments rob you of your peace and your joy.

- Resentments hurt you physically, emotionally and spiritually.

- There are three tests to determine if you have resentment.

o The Blame test; Are you blaming someone else or something else for your resentment?

o The Bitterness test; Are you having bad thoughts whenever you see a certain person or remember a certain event?

o The Behavior test; How do you behave around a certain person?

13) When a person said to John Wesley: "I can't forgive that person." Wesley replied: "I hope you never sin."

14) We can't just enjoy forgiveness we need to employ forgiveness.

15) The hallmark of Christianity is forgiveness. Am I really a Christian?

16) We have two choices:

    a) Continue to rehearse it repeatedly.

    b) Release it.

17) Release it - it's gone forever; Hold on to it - it lasts forever.

18) Isn't it time to release that hurt. Get that heaviness off you. Remove another obstacle or barrier to peace in your life.

You may purchase a tape of this message from Good News Christian Center. Through the Internet they may be contacted at

www.GoodNewsChristianCenter.org

or

at the following address:

815 Lee Street, DesPlaines, IL 60016

Phone (847) 390-5840

Cost is $4.00 plus shipping

APPENDIX F –
Lay Speakers Role in Renewal/
Revival Worship in the Local Church

For the Advanced Lay Speaker's Academy in the Northern Illinois Conference of the United Methodist Church, I developed this six-session course, which was held in the spring of 2000. While this course was presented to Certified Lay Speakers, it is applicable for everyone. Remember that we all are ministers, or comforters, in the kingdom of God. Therefore, it could be titled, <u>Your</u> Role in Renewal/Revival Worship in the Local Church. This course provides an insight into the current situation in some local churches concerning the style of worship and an alternative style of worship to provide spiritual skills for bringing about spiritual growth. Many churches are using this more contemporary format for Saturday evening services. Such a time frame allows the Saturday attendee to sleep in on Sunday morning.

This course also provides insight into how to bring about renewal/revival in the local church in a non-threatening manner. It encourages the thought that it is all right to be different, provided our vision is focused on God, our ears tuned to the voice of Christ and we are walking under the direction and discipline of the Holy

Spirit. It demonstrates that there is room for traditional worship, evangelical worship and even charismatic worship, without any worshiper compromising their faith in God. This course teaches lay speakers (and all who want to be used by God for His ministry; remember we are all ministers) to be aware of the "red flags" that are waved from many quarters that cool spiritual response to the word of God.

Each session provides hands-on skills to accomplish a phase of developing renewal and spiritual growth. Most importantly, it teaches how to address the subject of renewal/revival with the local pastor and church leaders without raising "red flags" that create misunderstanding and negative response. The course reviews many attributes that are essential for successful ministry in the area of renewal/revival.

Text for the course:

> Robb, E. W. "The Spirit Who Will Not Be Tamed" (The Wesleyan Message and The Charismatic Experience). © 1997 by E.W. Robb; Published by Bristol Books an imprint of Bristol House, Ltd., Anderson, IN 46013.

Other references are noted in the "References Used In 'Who Needs A Comforter?'" section at the end of this book.

Outline:

Session 1- What is renewal and revival? Why is it important?

Read chapters 1 and 2 in textbook.

A- Why is the 14 - 30 age group leaving the church? (Gallop)

B- How can this attitude be changed?

C- What can we do, as Lay Speakers, to modify this trend?

D- Small group discussion on these questions and possible solutions.

Session 2- Substance and Symbolism In A Renewal/Revival Worship Service

Read chapters 3 and 4 of textbook.

A- Traditional worship - What does it provide?

B- How can we change the symbolism in our worship to enhance spiritual substance?

C- Review of other seminars that are available such as Lay Witness Mission, Discover God's Call, Weekend of Discovery, Life in the Spirit Seminar and Alpha Course.

D- Small group discussion exploring the differences.

Session 3- Worship and Praise- Something For Everyone!

Read chapters 5 and 6 of textbook.

A- How can we bring these two words together without offending people who cling to different forms of worship?

B- What is classical and contemporary Christian music? How do they differ? When do you use both of these?

C- The biblical perspective of praise and worship. How musical instruments play a role.

D- A creative response to reaching the unchurched and the "X" generation.

Session 4- Prayer: Prayer Teams and Their Importance

Read chapters 7 and 8 of textbook.

A- The role of prayer in spiritual growth and healing.

B- Training prayer teams - Dos and Don'ts!

C- Listening To God!

Session 5- Lay Speakers (Your) Role in Promoting, Organizing and Assisting in a Renewal/Revival Program

Read chapters 9 and 10 of textbook.

A- Ways to handle doubts and opposition.

B- Prayer and organization spells success or disaster.

C- Format and leadership.

D- Small groups to plan a renewal/revival service.

Session 6- Experiencing A Renewal and Revival Service

Read chapters 11, 12 and 13 in textbook.

A- Answer any questions that have not been answered before.

B- Re-emphasize the highlights of the past 5 sessions.

C- Do It!! Hold an actual renewal/revival service.

It helps to experience IT, …. to pass IT on!!

If you would like to have more information please contact the author.

APPENDIX G -
"The Cilley Man"

Written and sung by Michael Papierski
for Charlie Cilley.

Chorus:

He's a dancing fool, a fool for Christ,.
Spirit filled, electrified.
Tellin' the world, about God's own Son,
Led by Faith, he's getting' it done.
Sleeps fully dressed, with a clip on tie,
Awaiting God's call, he's got the Spirit on-line.
Anointing and healing, and laying on hands,
Radically saved, he's the Cilley man.

You can find him in the church,
You can find him on the street.
Livin' God's Word,
And feeding God's sheep.
Housing the homeless,
And leading the lost.
Bringing them all,
To the foot of Christ's Cross.

He's the Deacon of the Dance,
He's the Broker we revere.
He'll sell you on Jesus,
Just lend him your ear.
Sinners are saved,
Not by his own hand,
But "By the grace of God",
Says the Cilley man.
"By the grace of God",
Says the Cilley man.

Chorus:

Instrumental Bridge:

He's an inspiration to all who claim Christ,
I'm proud to say that he's a brother of mine.

Chorus:

Radically saved,
He's the Cilley man.
Radically saved,
He's a silly man…

You may listen to this song sung by Michael Papierski at www.faithsong.org which is Michael's free website. Michael shares his thoughts and experiences that inspired this song on his website.

Michael states, "Charlie Cilley accepted Christ at fifty years of age and he's been trying to make up for lost time ever since. I have known few men so passionate about spreading the "Good News". Charlie seems locked into the Holy Spirit and I admire him for that. He is always ready and willing to act upon the Spirit's leading at any time, day or night. It seems as if every time I would see Charlie, he would be wearing a tie. One day I chided him about that, then grabbed his tie and yanked it. To my surprise, Charlie's clip-on tie ended up in my hand. Charlie just laughed. I appreciate his healing ministry and his desire to have every Christian receive the Holy Spirit into their heart."

I appreciate Michael's kind words and this original song. I will take the liberty of correcting the timetable of my life, as it is mentioned by Michael. It was at age 9 that I accepted Jesus Christ as Lord, Savior and Master, as evidenced by water baptism. It was at age 50 that I received the baptism of the Holy Spirit, as evidenced by resting in the Spirit. Michael was correct that I'm trying to make up for lost time – time from age 9 to age 50.

Does 40 years in the wilderness sound familiar? I was there! Michael's other songs may be heard on his web site. For more information on Michael Papierski, read his biography at www.faithsong.org.

APPENDIX H –
You Can Determine What You Receive from God

Pastor Tim Roames of Good News Christian Center gave this message on January 22, 2006. Pastor Tim started this message by saying that the title may sound anti-religious but it is not anti-God. Remember my definition of the difference between religion and Christianity: Religion is a belief in a doctrine and Christianity is a personal relationship with Jesus Christ. The following is a brief outline of his presentation.

TITLE: "You Can Determine What You Receive From God"

1) The Old Testament says: "… choose for yourself this day whom you will serve…" (See Joshua 24:14 -15)

Is it going to be blessings or curses? Mark 16:15-16; Matthew 7:7-8; Proverbs 8:17; Hebrews 11:6

2) God makes things easy; evil makes things hard.

3) There are four things you can do to determine what you receive. Pastor Tim used the story of the woman with the blood issue as stated in Mark 5:25-34.

A) Speak in Faith

B) Act on your belief

C) Receive your blessing

D) Tell about it.

4) Speak in Faith

She believed Jesus was a healer, Mark 5:28 and she spoke it.

If I love my wife but never say so, how will she know it? I must speak it.

5) Act on your belief

Mark 5: 27; It is not good enough to just talk about it. We must act on it.

What are your beliefs?

I believe God answers prayer.

I believe Jesus was an example.

I believe God heals.

Do you believe giving brings blessings?

Do you believe forgiving others can bring blessings to you?

> *"Keep your eyes on God"- seek thee first the kingdom of God and all else will be added unto you. Refer to Matthew 6:33.*

Super Bowl is not more important than Super God.

"Don't just say it - Do it!"

6) Receive your blessing.

Mark 5: 29; After she said it and acted on it, she received.

Most people want feelings and healing first before they give thanks. Points 4 & 5 above emphasize that we must speak in faith and act on our belief, sometimes even before we see results. Feelings and symptoms will occur after you speak and act upon it. Be sure to give thanks to God for your healing.

Just like there was power around Jesus, there is an unseen power in this room. Of course, Jesus' power is here, BUT it is just like the radio waves that are here. We must have the proper receptor to pick up that power.

7) Tell about it. Mark 5:33

Tell people how blessed you are. Benny Hinn says 80% of people who have been healed do not keep their healing, because they do not tell others about it.

8) The battle is the Lord's. I Samuel 17:45 – 54.

9) What do you need from God? God wants you to come home! Refer to Luke 15:18 – 24.

10) It is up to you; you choose.

You may purchase a tape of this message from Good News Christian Center. Through the Internet they may be contacted at www.GoodNewsChristianCenter.org or they can be contacted by mail or phone at the following address:

815 Lee Street

DesPlaines, IL 60016

Phone (847) 390-5840

Cost of a tape is $4.00 plus shipping (as of 2007)

APPENDIX I –
Television Programs Can Be Beneficial

Can You Forgive?

I just watched a television program about a prisoner serving an extended sentence for armed robbery. His three sons turned him in to the authorities. They were guests on the show. Later on in my comments, you'll see why this program was so meaningful to me from many different directions.

This experience is another indication of how we can be writing a new page everyday in our Book of Acts, our own Acts 29. The book of Acts is a biblical expression of the apostles' encounters within God's kingdom. The Bible contains only 28 chapters in the book of Acts. We, personally and individually, should be having our own encounters within God's kingdom. Hence, when we write down these encounters, they will become our own Acts 29.

When the talk show spokesperson asked the inmate how he felt about his sons turning him into the authorities he said, "What they did was right in their minds but it would have been better if they had come to me, confronted me and then let me turn myself in."

Later on in the program the inmate indicated that if he was a pedophile, a sexual offender, or any other kind of criminal that injured someone personally, then the sons would have been justified in turning him in. However, in his case, he came to no conclusions.

In Chapter 4, I wrote about Project Understanding Bail Project (PUBP). It is one of the organizations that Marj and I have been involved with for over 30 years. It was through this organization that I had the opportunity, and felt an obligation at that time, to help an individual turn himself in to the authorities. Whether he was guilty or not was not up to me to decide but it was up to the courts. In the final analysis, he has been sentenced to 70 years in prison for manslaughter.

I completely understand where the inmate is coming from when he says it would have been better for the boys to confront him and let him turn himself in. I have been there; I have experienced a similar situation, so is that much easier for me to understand? Timeout, I've just had to take a break as the tears were getting in the way.

I would like to comment about several other statements that were made during the show.

1- The inmate said to the sons- "Don't do as I do, but do as I say."

My Comments: This reminded me of many days during my PUBP activities, I would say to myself and to many of our clients, "There goes I but by the grace of God". Many of you know what I'm talking about. Except for the fact that we did not get caught, we may have been just as guilty as some of our PUBP clients.

2- The talk show spokesperson asked "Why did you do it?"

The inmate's response was "I felt all used up."

My Comments: Many of our clients in PUBP likewise felt like there was no other place to go because of their circumstances in life. Unfortunately many of our responses to life circumstances happen spontaneously and are based upon previous experiences or our foundational beliefs. Since many people have a very shaky foundation in their up-bringing it is very easy to be swayed to the illegal activities

3- "If you cry, you lose" was a family saying.

My Comments: This was very well demonstrated throughout the entire show. Yes, there were facial expressions of disgust and anger, but there was no crying during the show. I cried for them and I'm sure that God was crying too. God is a very compassionate God. It was very difficult to sit through this program without feeling compassion for the hurting people- all of the people involved. This includes mother, father, sons, relatives, the other woman and the victims of the robberies. Everyone who found themselves involved in the inmate's life in one way or another, undoubtedly was affected in some manner and was hurt.

4- One final comment made to the inmate was: "God is not the one that you injured."

My Comments: I understand from a secular point of view what was meant. However, from a spiritual point of view, our Creator, our Heavenly Father, must first forgive us before we can ask and receive forgiveness from another human being. After the program, I was trying to talk to my wife about this and, of course, being very emotional at times, the tears were flowing and interfering with our discussion. However, it reminded me of a question I ask many people. When you have a headache what do you do first? Most people answer that they take an aspirin or Tylenol. I would like to suggest that we should first say a word of prayer. Take the Gos-pills, (Gospels) first. If that doesn't work, then take the aspirin or Tylenol. I believe the inmate was correct in asking forgiveness from God first. I suggest that the sons need to do the same. Talk to the Heavenly Father first and then perhaps they can talk to their dad, their earthly father. If you get right with God first then everything else will fall into place.

> *"But seek first His kingdom and His righteousness, and all these things will be given to you as well".*
> *(Matthew 6:33 NIV)*

This program spoke to my heart because of my experiences with PUBP clients.

Human Relations And Low Self-esteem

Another excellent television program concerned human relations. Many such programs explore people's low self-esteem and how people deal with it. Such was this particular program, it focused on parents and their children who were having difficulty relating to other people.

One parent commented that they did not want their child to be hurt as they were. Which one was hurting the most? Both were suffering from insecurity. Both were feeling that they were not good enough. It was said that this was a form of generational curse, where the same thing happens repeatedly to three or four successive generations.

Unfortunately, in many cases, we **do** pass on our insecurities to our children. That can become a generational curse. However, prayer can break these generational curses. Furthermore, God has no grandchildren and therefore we are each responsible for our relationship with our heavenly Father. According to the Bible, there can also be generational blessings.

> *"You shall not make for yourself an idol in the form of anything in heaven above or on the earth beneath or in the waters below. You shall not bow down to them or worship them; for I, the Lord your God, am a jealous God, punishing the children for the sin of the fathers to the third and fourth generation of those who hate me, but showing love to a thousand generations of those who love me and keep my commandments." (Deuteronomy 5 :8 – 10 NIV)*

I Am Not Worthy

Another excellent television program had three individuals with different but surprisingly similar problems. The first guest was suffering with anorexia. The second guest was an obese woman and the third person could not spend money on herself.

The common threads that each shared were that

- All of the situations have a starting point.
- All of the women were told lies and they chose to believe them.

- The "old script" had been played over and over.
- In one way or another, they had all been rejected.
- They felt that I am not worthy or I am not good enough.
- They all had self-hatred.

Several great points were made during the program.

1- Obesity and anorexia are the flip side of the same coin.

2- When we have children, we give up our right to self-destruct.

3- Healing occurs when we can rewrite the script.

4- You must get inside yourself, not beside yourself.

My Comments

God doesn't make junk, people make junk. God <u>made</u> you and His plan is purposeful. You are not junk! Do not hate yourself. The women of this program hated themselves because of lies that others had told them. They bought into the lies; they bought the hatred and their lives became junk. Don't let this happen to you!

In addition, you can't survive on your own. We all need someone to help us through life. Jesus Christ did not live His life on his own and you can't either. We need God. Many of us have burdens that we have been carrying for several years. It is time to release them to the Lord. When you release your burdens, there is undoubtedly a void in your heart. That void needs to be filled or the hurt will come back. When hurt returns it often brings many of its friends - jealousy, resentment, hatred, anger, rage, and distrust. The best way that I know to fill the void is to receive the infilling of the Holy Spirit.

Ask the Lord to be your Savior, live by His word, and seek the power of the Holy Spirit.

APPENDIX J –
Vision of a Sign Given to
Oral Roberts

The following is reprinted from the Introduction of *The Wake-Up Call.*

> *"In the last half of 2004, God released through his servant Oral Roberts a vision of a sign He would give to alert mankind to the Second Coming of Jesus. God told Brother Roberts He was giving men and women a wake-up call to make sure they are ready. ..... Do whatever is necessary in your life to be ready- right now! Let this vision be your Wake-up call."*
> *(p. 3-4)*

The following is reprinted from Part 1, *Believers Voice of Victory* of *The Wake-Up Call* Broadcast, September 27-30, 2004.

"....**Richard:** This is a very special time because God has given a vision to my father – a vision of about the future of this nation, of the Jews, of the Christians, of the world -- and what God is about to do. And God has given Kenneth a prophetic word concerning that vision, which is extremely important to you and you don't want to miss what's going to happen. The Bible says in Amos 3:7: 'Surely the Lord God does nothing, unless He reveals His secrets to His servants the prophets' *(New King James Version).*

"**Kenneth:** Amen.

"**Richard:** And I want you to listen with your heart, because I believe when you hear the vision and you hear the prophetic interpretation you're going to be touched. You're going to know what God is about to do. You can get your heart ready and be prepared, and it's important for us to be prepared. Dad, would you just begin to share the vision that God has laid on your heart?

"**Oral:** In the midst of the turmoil, the fear, the anxiety that's in our nation and in our world, as I was walking and meditating, I heard the voice of God. I've heard that voice many times. It's familiar to me, and there's no way that I can fail to understand it's His voice because I'm familiar with it. And instantly I heard that voice and I heard it and then I saw with my eyes something I'd never seen, suddenly, in the clouds in the skies above New York City and the east part of the United States, and which hung there for quite some time and then spread out across America, without touching the ground, and then God diffused it away from America and sent it out to the nations of the earth. And I saw and I heard. What did I see? I saw something coming down from above: smoke and vapor and blood – or it looked like that to my eyes, to my spiritual eyes. There it was hanging so huge until it almost blotted out the sky. Instantly I thought about 9/11, when the terrorist attacked the Twin Towers and through television all of us in America, and probably the world, saw those more than a hundred– story high buildings crumple and heard the cry of thousands of people who were being either killed or wounded. I remembered the fear that struck my heart and knew that what I was feeling everybody else was feeling and remembered that never in the history of the world, and certainly not of America, that something of this proportion had struck the human race and was a preview of things similar to it that were going to happen through what we now call terrorists. First, I saw this thing hovering and great changes coming in it to where I couldn't miss it. And then I heard, something came into my ears, and it reminded me of what a friend of mine had said when the first space capsule was released into the sky. They told me that they made of all of them- he was a newsman in New York City- to be maybe half mile or more away from the capsule. And he said when that thing lifted off the earth, there was a sound, and the sound itself moved the weeds and the growth, and he said, 'It penetrated my body.' He said, 'As I talked to others, they felt the same thing.' He said the sound was so enormous that nothing had ever happened like it in the history of the world. Instantly, I thought of that because the sound that was coming into my ears was penetrating my whole being. And then I heard God's voice. He said, 'I'm making a sign. This is a sign according to the second chapter of Acts, where the Apostle Peter, upon the giving of the Holy Spirit, the Baptism of the Holy Spirit, said there'll be signs in the skies.' He said, 'This is one of the signs of the end time because the world is not ready for the Second Coming of My Son.' He said, 'My Church is not ready for the Second Coming of My Son.' He said, 'The Jews, with whom I've had the covenant for thousands of years, they're not ready for the Second Coming of My Son.' He said, 'The nations of the earth are not ready for the Second Coming of My Son.' He said, 'America has been set aside by a special covenant that I made with many of the people who came to found this nation several hundred years ago, that this was My nation and the gospel was going to go out from it unlike any other nation and there'd be more gospel going out from America.' And He said, not only would there be a powerful military presence in the United States unlike any other nation, but it would be the center of the gospel that I was sending out. And He said to me, 'You remember that I said in My Bible to My disciples 2000 years ago, 'Go into all the world and teach all nations, and when that teaching has reached the nations then shall the end come.' And then he startled me.

He said, 'With all of the widespread force of My Church in the world, but particularly in the United States, which is the source of most of the gospel that's being preached in all the world,' He said, 'there is a wasting of My power, there is a failure to grasp the end times. And the Church, they are coming to church on Sunday morning mostly for themselves. And the preachers, for the most part, are not really concerned about the nations of the earth. They're concerned about the little group that is there, and they sing their songs and they get up and preach.' And [He] said, 'When 9/11 struck, there was a fear that came into the hearts, even of My people of the Church and of people outside the Church. And millions the following Sunday or two rushed to go to church. But the preachers were not prepared, and most of them didn't even preach on it and didn't even talk about it being the sign of something that's coming hundreds of thousands of times bigger.' He said, 'When those planes of the terrorists struck the Twin Towers in New York City and they gradually came tumbling down, it was something bigger than people had ever seen, but it's nothing in comparison to what's going to happen in the Second Coming of My Son.' And so He said, 'My Church was not prepared to deal with that, and people came to church and then nothing much happened and they dropped back and many of them went back to their bars,' as I heard Kenneth Copeland say. 'And there

I was with My whole creation that's alive in the earth, not counting all those who have died – millions who have lived and died, all of whom will be resurrected at some time in the future, having to do with the Second Coming of My Son, some to everlasting life, some to live forever in their new bodies and some to everlasting shame and contempt forever lost.' And He said, I love people. I created them. I love them by creation. I love them because I sent My only begotten Son.' And instantly I thought of the great show that Mel Gibson made of "The Passion."

"**Kenneth:** Yes

"**Oral:** When millions upon millions went to see it and are seeing it now all over the world. I remember when I sat there with my wife, watching it, and how my soul was stirred and the tears sprang from my eyes and my body trembled as I saw something about the sufferings of Jesus, the Son of God, to save the human race and so that the devil would not destroy God's creation. He would not destroy men, women and children that God had created and for whom Jesus had died and rose from the dead that we might be born again - we might repent of our sins and have salvation and come into a readiness for the coming of Christ. And He says, 'As you know in the Bible, the Second Coming is in two parts. One is called the Rapture, one is called the revelation. And first of all I'm going to rapture, or catch up, My people – the people who are born of My Spirit and filled with My Spirit and serving Me. I'm going to catch them up in a moment of time and they'll meet My Son in the clouds and come on into heaven, into My presence. And then not long after, I'm going to bring that bride of Christ back with Jesus when He comes the second time to the earth, and that'll be the beginning of the judgment of the nations.' But He said, 'The thing that is breaking My heart is that I commanded My people, I commanded My Church to preach the gospel in all the world and to teach all nations. And while there are evangelists and pastors and prophets and apostles and all kinds of My workers in various parts of the world and in some of the nations of the earth, it's just a drop in the bucket to what I commanded My disciples to do. And I love people so much I cannot afford to let people go on like they are.' Then He directed my attention to the book of Matthew, the 24th chapter, where He speaks in the 24th chapter and beginning at verse 35: 'Heaven and earth shall pass away, but my words shall not pass away. But of that day and hour knoweth no man, no, not the angels of heaven, but my Father only.' What I'm talking about is known only to the Father. 'But as the days of Noah were, so shall also the coming of the Son of man be. For as the days that were before the flood that – there was eating and drinking – eating and drinking, marrying and giving in marriage, until the day that Noah entered into the ark, and knew not until the flood came; And the coming – so shall the coming of the Son of man be.' Now, He reminded me in the sixth chapter of Genesis that the earth was filled with violence and it was so full it couldn't be any more full and it grieved the heart of God that He had made man and He decided that He would destroy man and begin over, and He established a remnant and it was a family, Noah and his family. And He commanded him to build a huge boat that would take two of every living thing in it so when the Flood came – and they'd never had rain before in the earth, it had been watered by a mist. But 'when,' He said, 'when the flood comes and this boat with this family and two of every living thing gets in it and the flood lifts them up from the earth that's being destroyed, or from the human race that's being destroyed, the flood that lifts the ark, or the remnant of My people, in Noah's day, will come down in judgment upon the people of the earth.' And He said, 'Now, there's got to be preaching with fire in the belly. There's got to be Anointing of the Holy Ghost. My Church has to wake up because what I'm revealing in this sign that every eye is going to see, every ear is going to hear. They'll see this thing. They will not necessarily know what it is, but it's a wake-up call about the Second Coming of My Son. It's not going to come and touch the earth. It's going to be seen, it's going to be heard, and people are going to become aware of the drama of the end time, of the Second Coming of Christ. When He splits the skies and comes back with His bride and takes over the reign of the earth and He destroys the Antichrist, who will arise at that time. He will destroy the followers of Antichrist and He'll establish His kingdom upon the earth.' And He said, 'I cannot let anybody live and die without knowledge that My Son is coming back the second time.'

"Well, I shook in my body. I went into the kitchen where Evelyn, my darling wife was, and I immediately told her. The following day my son, Richard, flew out from Tulsa to California, where I now live in the sunset of my life. I'm now 86 and Evelyn is 87. And I set him down and I told him what I've told you. Then I picked up the phone and I called a prophet of God, Kenneth Copeland, who is my son in the Lord for, I guess, 45 years at least – a powerful man of God in this earth and in the world. And I told him what I've told you. And then I said, 'Kenneth, it seems to me that we should tell the world about this vision,' because I saw it and I heard it and I know that sometime – well, it seems to me it could be very soon – that this sign, whatever form it is revealed to you, maybe you won't see it exactly like I saw it, but you'll see something that's beyond anything you've ever seen. You'll hear something in the innermost part of your being that you've not heard. It'll have to do with the

Second Coming, to tell you it's now time to get on your knees. I feel it now coming out of my being. It's now time to go back to church. But it's now time, preacher, teacher, to get up with my Bible and really preach the Second Coming of Christ and to tell people things aren't going on like they're going on now. There's going to be an end of all this. There's going to be a wake-up of the whole world, and the terrorists are just the prelude. What we're seeing now from them is not going to stop. There are going to be things happen from them that's beyond what we now see, and I'll say more about that in a moment. But, Richard and Kenneth, I tell you again as I've already done a few days ago, that's the vision that God gave me." (p. 5-16)

Reprinted with permission from Kenneth Copeland Ministries.

NOTE: The complete transcript of the prophecy program is available from Kenneth Copeland Ministries as *The Wake-Up Call* mini book. More information is available at www.kcm.org or call 1-800- 600- 7395 or write to: Kenneth Copeland Ministries

Fort Worth, Texas, 76192-0001

Author's Comments:

When the *Believers Voice of Victory* broadcast was on TV from September 27 through October 8, 2004, I was attentive in listening to every word, as it was confirmation of what I had been working on for two years. This vision and prophecy of Oral Roberts was confirmation of what God had been telling me.

I was also hearing: "My people are not ready for the second coming of My Son, Jesus Christ."

More specifically, that they (His people) had not received the Holy Spirit in all its <u>fullness</u>, as God, the Father had intended, as seen in Acts 1: 4-5 & 8 (the Promised Gift and Power from the Father) and as Jesus told us in John 14:15-30. Jesus promised us another Counselor to be with us forever, the Spirit of Truth. Jesus also told us in verse 27 that He would give us His Peace. WHY don't we have peace in more <u>fullness</u> than we do? I believe it is because we have NOT received the Holy Spirit as God has available to us.

These books, *The Wake-Up Call* mini book and *Who Needs A Comforter?,* I believe, should be a wake-up call for all of us, Christians and non-Christians. We, ALL, should heed the warning of God!

Solution To Puzzle In Chapter 14

Clue- "This causes one to think outside the normal boundaries that society and worldly education puts around us."

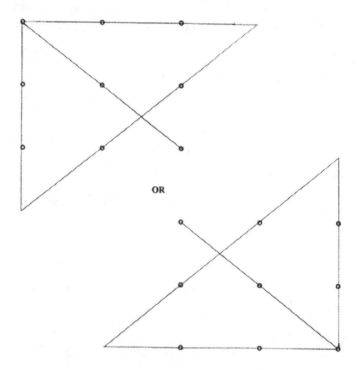

OR

You MUST go outside the box that your mind has set as "normal boundaries" !

Scriptural References
used throughout the book

All New International Version (NIV) except where noted

Chapter 1

Hosea 4:6

Acts 1:8

John 14:25-26

John 14:27

Chapter 2

II Corinthians 5:17

Acts 10:34-35

II Timothy 3:16-17

Job 32:8

Chapter 6

Hebrews 13:5b

Chapter 7

Song of Songs 2 4

Chapter 8

Romans 15:13

Acts 1:4-5

Romans 15:13

John 14:25-27

Chapter 9

Acts9:3-4

John 18:4-6

Acts 1:4

Mark 6:5

Mark 8:25

Acts 28:8b

Acts 8:14-17

John 3:5

Acts 1:5

Exodus 30:23-25

Chapter 10

Ephesians 5:20

Song of Songs 2: 4

I John 4:4

Chapter 11

Exodus 20:4-6

Chapter 12

John 14:6

Romans 10:9-10

Romans 10:10

Acts 1:4-5

I Peter 5:7

John 14:27

Acts 1:8a

Luke 3:15

John 14:27 (Living Bible)

Mark 1:4

Mark 1:7-8

Luke 3:4

John 3:3-8

Luke 3:16b

Chapter 13

John 14:16-17

Matthew 17:20b-21

John 17:22-24

John 14:27a

Galatians 5:22-23a

Appendix A

Luke 11:13

Acts 1:8

Appendix I
   Matthew 6:33
   Deuteronomy 5: 8-10

Appendix J
   Amos 3:7 (King James Version
   Matthew 24:35 (King James Version)

Other scriptures may be mentioned in the Appendixes by the contributing writers.

References

Preface

Hagee, J. (2006). *Jerusalem countdown*. Lake Mary, FL: Strange Communications Co. ISBN 9781591858935

Unknown (producer). (2005, May 20). *Resurrection* [Television broadcast, Chicago]. ABC Television Network: www.ABCnewsstore.com

Chapter 1

Kimmel, Alea Joy of Des Plaines, IL., Original sketches of electrical plugs; Permission granted for use May 19, 2007.

Chapter 2

Bethel, J. P. General Editor. (1961). *Webster's New Collegiate Dictionary*. Springfield, Massachusetts: G&C Merrian Co.

Chapter 3

Evans, A. T. (Senior Pastor, Oak Cliff Bible Fellowship). (2002). *The Rookie Demon* on The Alternative with Dr. Tony Evans [Radio broadcast]. Dallas, TX.

Harvey, P. (Editorial commentator). *If I were the devil* [Radio broadcast]. ABC Radio Networks.

Morris, W. (1975). *American Heritage Dictionary: New College Edition.* Boston: American Heritage Publishing Co. & Houghton Mifflin Company

Packer, J. I. (1993). *Knowing God.* Westmont, IL: Inter-Varsity Press. ISBN 0-8308-1650-X

Tada, J. E. & Estes, S. (1990). *A Step Further.* Grand Rapids, MI: Zondervan Publishing Co. ISBN 10-0310239710

United Methodist Hymnal. (1989). Song by Gaither; W. J. (1971). *He Touched Me.* Nashville, TN: The United Methodist Publishing House.

Chapter 4

Aldersgate Renewal Ministries. www.aldersgaterenewal.org Permission granted for use: December 8, 2006

Full Gospel Business Men Fellowship International. www.fgbmfi.org

Promise Keepers. www.promisekeepers.org

United Methodist Church. (1976). *Guidelines: The United Methodist Church and the Charismatic Movement.* Nashville, TN: Discipleship Resources.

Chapter 5

Hudson, J. (1997, November 15). The Messenger. *UMC newsletter*. Permission granted for use September 12, 2005.

Hudson, S. [Testimony of Susan Hudson]. Permission granted for use September 12, 2005.

Chapter 6

Chickering, D. [personal communication]. Permission granted for use February 10, 2006.

Heavenly Inspiration. (2005, August 4). *Des Plaines Times*.

Kimmel, Alea Joy of Des Plaines, IL., [Testimony of the artist – Alea Joy Kimmel]; Permission granted for use May 19, 2007.

Chapter 7

Worship Conference. (2003, February 9). Aldersgate Renewal Ministries. (Audiotape).

Chapter 8

Schlatterer, E. (2005). [Personal Testimony] Permission granted for use May 31, 2005. ten Boom, C. (1977). *Each New Day*. Westwood, NJ: Barbour & Co., Inc. ISBN 0-916441-20-2

Chapter 10

Brennan, J. Illinois Bone and Joint Institute Physical Therapy Program. [personal communication]. Permission granted for use April 2007.

Cwanek, C. [personal communication]. Permission granted for use August 7, 2006.

Evangelical Sisterhood of Mary, Canaan in the Desert. Phoenix, AZ. Permission granted for use April 17, 2007.

Touching The Nations. www.touchingthenations.com

Chapter 11

Morris, W. (1975). *American Heritage Dictionary: New College Edition.* Boston: American Heritage Publishing Co. & Houghton Mifflin Company

Schlatterer, E. [personal correspondence]. Permission granted for use May 31, 2005.

Seamands, D. (1985). *Healing of Memories.* Wheaton, IL: Victor Books of SP Publications, Inc. ISBN 0-89693-532-9

Chapter 12

Jones, Rev. E. Stanley. (1955, 1992 as an Abingdon Classic). *Mastery: The art of mastering life*. Nashville, TN: Abingdon Press. ISBN 0-687-23734-3 Adapted by Permission, November 20, 2006

Appendix A

Roames, Pastor Timothy. (2004, December 5). *Welcoming the Holy Spirit into Your Life Is a Wise and Powerful Thing to Do* (Audiotape). Permission granted for use August 2, 2006.

Appendix E

Roames, Pastor Timothy. (2005, June 5). *Prayer of Release* (Audiotape). Permission granted for use August 2, 2006.

Appendix F

Barna, G. (1988). *Marketing the church: What they never taught you about church growth*. Colorado Springs, CO: Navpress.

Cho, P. Y. (1984). *Prayer: Key to revival*. Dallas, TX: Word Publishing. ISBN 0-8499-3073-1

Flessing & Flessing. (Producers). (1996, June 28-29). Chicago Conference: *Break down the walls* [video]. (Distributed by Promise Keepers, Denver, CO)

Fresh Air Media. (Producer). (1999). *Hope for a new millennium* [video]. (Distributed by Promise Keepers, Denver, CO)

Gallop, G. (1989). *The people's religion: American faith in the 90's*. New York: MacMillan Publishing Co.

Graham, B. (1998). *The Holy Spirit: Activating God's power in your life*. Dallas, TX: Word Publishing. ISBN 0-8499-3072-3

Lavin Company, Inc. (Producer). (1997). *Go inside the Toronto blessing* [video]. (Distributed by Fresh Start Marketing, Inc., Canton, OH 44709)

Odyssey Productions Ltd. (Producer). (1998). *Landmarks of faith. Methodist camp meetings: A travelogue of American spirituality* [video]. (Distributed by Goldhil Video, Thousand Oaks, CA.)

Robb, E. W. (1997). The Spirit Who Will Not Be Tamed. *The Wesleyan Message and the Charismatic Experience*. Anderson, IN: Bristol Books. ISBN: 1-885224-12-5

Sumrall, L.. (1993). *The gifts and ministries of the Holy Spirit*. Springdale, PA: Whitaker House. ISBN 0-88368-236-2

Appendix G

Papierski, M. (1998). *The Cilley Man*. (Original song) J. Halter/M. Papierski. Permission granted for use February 15, 2006

Appendix H

Roames, Pastor Timothy. (2006, January 22). *You Can Determine What You Receive From God*. (Audiotape message). Permission granted for use August 2, 2006

Appendix J

Copeland, K., Roberts, O., & Roberts, R. with commentary by Copeland, G. & Brim, B. (2004). *The Wake-Up Call*. Fort Worth, TX: Kenneth Copeland Publications. ISBN 1-57562-815-5